Fix Your Own Computer For Sen~~iors~~

~~FOR~~

DUMMIES®

by Corey Sandler
and Tom Badgett

WILEY

Wiley Publishing, Inc.

Fix Your Own Computer For Seniors For Dummies®

Published by
Wiley Publishing, Inc.
111 River Street
Hoboken, NJ 07030-5774

www.wiley.com

For general information on our other products and services, please contact our Customer Care Department within the U.S. at 877-762-2974, outside the U.S. at 317-572-3993, or fax 317-572-4002.

For technical support, please visit www.wiley.com/techsupport.

Wiley also publishes its books in a variety of electronic formats. Some content that appears in print may not be available in electronic books.

Library of Congress Control Number: 2009940282

ISBN: 978-0-470-50087-3

Manufactured in the United States of America

10   9   8   7   6   5   4   3   2

WILEY

About the Author

Corey Sandler is the author of more than a hundred books with more than two million copies in print in more than twenty languages. A former Gannett and Associated Press newsman, he has appeared on NBC's *Today* show, the Travel Channel, and National Public Radio, and has been profiled on CNN.

His fascination with the mystery of the life and death of Henry Hudson took him on a year-long, 25,000-mile journey to England, Norway, Svalbard, and the North Pole; up New York's Hudson River to its source, and deep into Canada's wilderness of Hudson Bay and James Bay.

Sandler lives on Nantucket island, off the coast of Massachusetts.

About the Contributing Author

Tom Badgett is a writer and entrepreneur. He founded one of the first national personal computer sales and programming companies in 1980. He was a founding owner of the tenth-largest Internet service provider in 1994 (U.S. Internet, now part of Earthlink), and was a founding partner in IdleAire Technologies Corporation, a national provider of HVAC, Internet, and other services for long-haul truck drivers.

Badgett is a prolific writer, having published more than 50 books and hundreds of magazine articles for major U.S. and international publishers on technical topics from computer software to computer communications and security. He produced more than 30 instructional videos and interactive DVD programs on similar topics, also marketed internationally. Badgett has worked as a magazine writer and technical editor (Ziff-Davis, McGraw-Hill), broadcast DJ, journalist and documentary producer for radio and television. He taught computer programming, journalism, photography, technical writing, and speech and theater at the college level for several years.

He holds a BA in language and an MA in documentary film from the University of Tennessee.

Author's Acknowledgements

Publishing is a team sport, and I had some great players and coaches all around. Thanks to Tonya Cupp, Katie Mohr, and Kathy Simpson for their professional work on moving this title from concept to print. And once again, to old friend Tom Badgett for coming off the bench to pinch-hit in a key moment of the game.

Author's Dedication

To my dad, now in his tenth decade, a senior amongst seniors.

Publisher's Acknowledgments

We're proud of this book; please send us your comments at http://dummies.custhelp.com. For other comments, please contact our Customer Care Department within the U.S. at 877-762-2974, outside the U.S. at 317-572-3993, or fax 317-572-4002.

Some of the people who helped bring this book to market include the following:

Acquisitions, Editorial

Project Editor: Tonya Maddox Cupp

Acquisitions Editors: Katie Mohr, Tiffany Ma

Copy and Development Editor: Kathy Simpson

Technical Editor: Sandy Berger

Editorial Manager: Jodi Jensen

Media Development Associate Producers: Josh Frank, Marilyn Hummel, Douglas Kuhn, and Shawn Patrick

Editorial Assistant: Amanda Graham

Sr. Editorial Assistant: Cherie Case

Cartoons: Rich Tennant (www.the5thwave.com)

Composition Services

Project Coordinator: Katherine Crocker

Layout and Graphics: Samantha K. Cherolis, Joyce Haughey, Christine Williams

Proofreader: Jacqui Brownstein

Indexer: BIM Indexing & Proofreading Services

Publishing and Editorial for Technology Dummies

    Richard Swadley, Vice President and Executive Group Publisher

    Andy Cummings, Vice President and Publisher

    Mary Bednarek, Executive Acquisitions Director

    Mary C. Corder, Editorial Director

Publishing for Consumer Dummies

    Diane Graves Steele, Vice President and Publisher

Composition Services

    Debbie Stailey, Director of Composition Services

Contents at a Glance

Table of Contents

*T*he way I look at being a senior is this: We got there ahead of the rest of the pack.

Let those behind us get all excited over tweets and iPods and video games that simulate the challenges and joys of life. We've been there before — before there were computers, as a matter of fact.

When the PC arrived it was hard to imagine what its ultimate role would be. We played some games, we used it to balance our checkbooks, and we learned to put aside our dumb typewriters and use the computer as something with a new title: a word processor.

And then everything began to come together. The computer was connected to the telephone system and through it to a completely new concept, the World Wide Web (now more commonly known as the Internet).

Through that connection, the computer became a carrier of a new kind of communication, called e-mail. And over the same wire (and its faster cousins including DSL and cable television connections) came Internet video, Internet radio, and digital images.

And though Sears no longer sends out its huge catalog, the Internet as the replacement for mail order has become a major part of commerce in our society. There is very little that you (and your credit card or an electronic link directly to your bank) cannot purchase online.

About This Book

The purpose of this book is not to point out how stupid you are. I don't believe that for a second . . . in fact, it is our generation that invented all of these great devices.

But it is also true that for some of us it is important to update our metaphors and clear out our mental attics so that we can function efficiently as seniors. I'll try to explain, in plain English, just enough about how a computer works to help you understand it. And, as promised in the book's title, I'll show you ways you can make simple repairs to your computer that will extend its life, save you money, and amaze the youngsters.

Foolish Assumptions

You have a computer and you want to fix a problem, prevent a problem, or be able to intelligently discuss your needs and wants with your 14-year-old grandson. Nothing foolish there. I also assume that you don't have an advanced degree in computer programming or electrical engineering. That's just fine.

The information in this book should be of use to any personal computer (PC) user. The differences between a desktop and a laptop, between a PC and a Mac, or between a machine running Microsoft Windows, Mac OS, or another operating system are not that great anymore.

But for the record, I assume the following as your standard machine:

➡ A PC.

➡ An Intel or AMD microprocessor (which together account for nearly all current processing units in PCs)

➡ A current version of the Microsoft Windows operating system (Windows XP, Windows Vista, or Windows 7)

➡ A current Web browser (Microsoft Internet Explorer, Mozilla Firefox, or other similar products, including Google Chrome)

Why You Need This Book

My children never knew a world without Nintendo or PCs or e-mail. I once told my daughter to make a "carbon copy" of something she was about to mail and she looked at me as if I had two heads. When I explained what I meant she rolled her eyes, and I felt very, very old.

But for the rest of us, the fact that we have a history (we remember life before Google, before YouTube, before cell phones) sometimes makes it harder to deal with the fast pace of change.

Just as you don't need to understand fuel injection or the chemistry of a catalytic convertor in order to drive your car to the post office, you also don't have to upgrade a chipset or decode a binary file to be able to use a personal computer.

But when it comes to making simple repairs or directing a service center to do them for you, it does help to know what those things are.

Conventions Used in This Book

This book uses certain conventions to highlight important information and help you find your way around, including these:

Icons

Helpful suggestions for tasks in the steps lists.

Potentially dangerous things to avoid.

Stuff you type

When you have to type something onscreen using the keyboard you'll see it in **bold**. Except for right now.

Figures

Many have notes or other markings to draw your attention to a specific part of the figure. The text tells you what to look for; the figure notes help you find it.

Menu commands

This arrow symbol ⇨ shows a sequence of steps on a computer menu. For example, Start⇨All Programs⇨Accessories means to click the Start button, click All Programs, and then click Accessories.

Options and buttons

Various versions of Windows use a mix of upper-and-lowercase, all uppercase, and even sOmetimes an odd construction like this one to indicate your options. If you're clicking on one of them, their style of presentation does not matter. (The sOmetimes example is the sort of thing that appears in some onscreen menus; it is meant to indicate that in addition to clicking on the words to choose them, you can use a keyboard combination like Alt plus the capitalized letter. In this instance, Alt+O would choose the sOmetimes option.)

How This Book Is Organized

This book is organized into logical sections, but you don't have to read it front to back.

Part 1: A Computer Is Not a Toaster

A toaster, or a bicycle, or a desk fan are each relatively complex pieces of technology. But when they stop browning bread, pushing the wheel, or blowing air the reason for their failure is usually very obvious. You can see the broken part and you might even be able to fix it with a screwdriver or a hammer. Alas, that's not the case with a computer. In Chapter 1, I show you how to get to know the parts you can see, like the mouse, keyboard, monitor, printer, and connection ports.

In Chapter 2, I take a tour inside the box, to help you understand the brain of your PC. And in Chapter 3, I introduce you to the operating system (Windows for most of us) and other major pieces of software.

Part II: Keeping Your PC Healthy with Preventive Maintenance

Here we explore healthy habits for you and your machine. In Chapter 4 you explore how to maintain, update, and repair Windows and software. In Chapter 5 it's time to read about proper computer hygiene, including keeping things clean and cool. In Chapter 6 it's time to think about dealing with evil-doers; I show you how to play defense against viruses, malware, and spam. In Chapter 7 I'll help you decide when and how to seek expert assistance and also give some pointers on weighing the cost of repair against the price of replacement of your PC or its major parts.

Part III: Fixing Sick Hardware

Does the hardware exist to run the software, or do you need software in order to use the hardware? It doesn't really matter; one is not much use without the other. In Chapter 8, we'll look into the display or monitor. In Chapter 9, I'll help you solve basic electrical and mechanical problems. In Chapter 10, I'll explain how to change or upgrade your PC's memory. In Chapter 11, I'll do the same for hard disk drives and CD or DVD drives. In Chapter 12 we'll consider ways to diagnose problems with a malfunctioning printer. And In Chapter 13 we'll explore good mousekeeping and other fixes for the mouse and keyboard.

Part IV: Resetting the Operating System

I've already posed the question of whether hardware or software is supreme. The fact is, though, that if the operating system becomes scrambled, the hardware will sit there like a cold pile of silicon and metal. In Chapter 14 I begin by explaining how to repair, refresh, and sometimes reinstall Windows. In Chapter 15 I help you examine and change system configuration. And in Chapter 16 I tell you how to restore your computer's settings back to the condition they were in the last time the PC worked properly.

Part V: Troubleshooting Your PC

You've got a problem; here are solutions that don't require a soldering iron, a doctoral degree, or the bratty neighbor kid. In Chapter 17 I'll show how to start your machine in Safe Mode, an important tool to make changes to an injured PC. In Chapter 18 we'll explore the Device Manager and Windows Troubleshooting Wizard, a pair of power tools that come with the operating system. Chapter 19 concentrates on fixing the soft side of hard disk drives, including fragmented files, disk errors, and other issues. In Chapter 20, I give a just-the-news roundup of fixes to common problems in a PC; these tricks of the trade are worth the price of admission.

Time to Get Started!

If you're a methodical type, start at the beginning and read about your PC before you attempt to prevent or correct problems. On the other hand, if you already know what's wrong, consult the table of contents or the index and jump right in to the section that deals with the problem.

And if you discover a solution not included here (or a problem not envisioned), I'd like to hear from you. Fire up your PC and send me an e-mail at `fixpc@econoguide.com`.

Part I

A Computer Is Not a Toaster

The 5th Wave   By Rich Tennant

THE SCARLET LETTER

©RICHTENNANT

17th CENTURY | 20th CENTURY

ADULTERY | ANALOG

Getting to Know the Parts You Can See

You wouldn't want a surgeon to operate without knowing the pertinent parts of the human body — especially if you're the patient. By the same token, you really shouldn't do surgery on your PC if you don't know what its components are and what they do.

Fortunately, hardware is more modular and less costly today than it was in the "good ole days," so most of the repairs or enhancements you want to make aren't necessarily difficult or highly technical. You just need to understand some basics about your computer's anatomy, and you should be good to go.

Another reason to know these basics: Whether or not you ever need to make repairs, understanding computer physiology should help you get more use out of your PC and make your experience with it less frustrating.

This chapter isn't the *Gray's Anatomy* of computers; for that, you need a more-in-depth book such as my *Fix Your Own PC* (Wiley Publishing). Think of the chapter as being a form of *CliffsNotes* — just enough to start with — and check out the cross-referenced chapters for more details.

Make a Point: Mice and Other Pointing Devices

A *pointing device* allows you to move a pointer onscreen to work directly with the elements you find there. Your PC may have some combination of the following:

➡ **Mouse:** This device gives your computer a hand, in a metaphorical sort of way. It's one of the most intuitive elements of a computer, easy to grasp and to use. See Chapter 13 for more on mice. You may have either of two kinds:

- **Wired:** The most common pointing device is the basic mouse (see **Figure 1-1**), which is about the size of a deck of cards. Its two buttons and long tail (connection wire) make it look vaguely mouselike. Some mice have three buttons or a small scroll wheel on top.

- **Wireless:** A wireless mouse has no tail; instead, it communicates with the computer via radio-frequency or infrared waves. You need to keep a wireless mouse fed (powered) with batteries.

➡ **Trackball:** Some users prefer a trackball (see **Figure 1-2**), which is essentially an upside-down mouse. You move the pointer onscreen by spinning the ball.

Left mouse button   Scroll wheel   Right mouse button

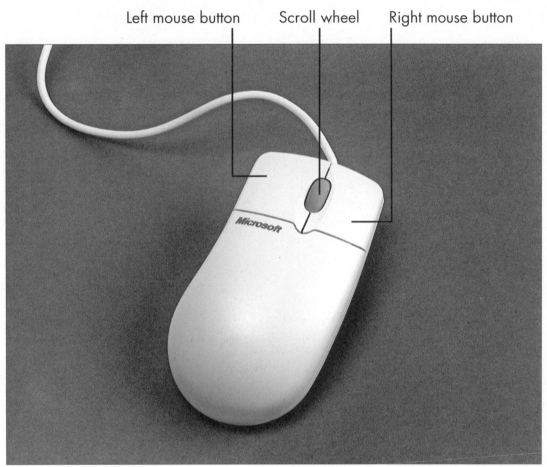

Figure 1-1

 The trackball is my preferred pointing device because it doesn't require much desk space and is also easier on the wrist and shoulder than a mouse is.

➡ **Touchpad:** Many PCs feature a touchpad, which is a matchbook-size, touch-sensitive screen on a laptop or a stand-alone device that plugs into a desktop computer. You move the pointer onscreen by pushing your finger along the touchpad.

Spin this ball to move the mouse pointer.

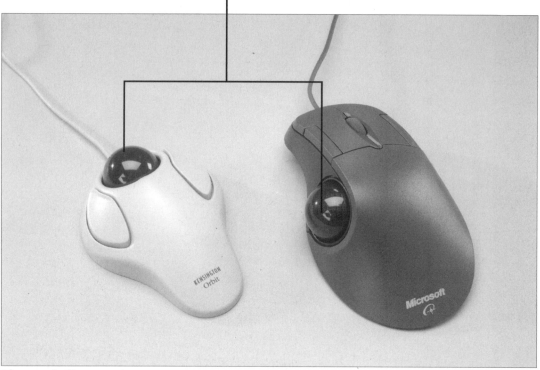

Figure 1-2

Stay on Key: Keyboards and Other Input Devices

➠ **Keyboard:** The keyboard (see **Figure 1-3**) is the one part of a computer that most of us have dealt with for nearly all of our lives. (Remember the typewriter? Its odd QWERTY layout for the keys is pretty much unchanged.) Like mice, keyboards come in two flavors: wired and wireless. I discuss keyboards in more detail in Chapter 13.

➠ **Tablet:** A *tablet* is a flat device — an active touchscreen (like that on a GPS receiver or an automated teller machine) or a metal or plastic pad — that allows you to interact with the computer in a way that resembles using a paper tablet or notebook.

Although tablet input devices have been around for a long time, they're still used mostly in high-end graphics stations and by folks who need to input precision drawing or graphics data. If, however, you need to input variable data and just like the concept of using a penlike stylus to interact with your PC, a tablet may be for you.

Special computer function keys

Familiar typewriter-style keys

Figure 1-3

See Clearly Now: Monitors

In this book, for simplicity's sake, I use the terms *monitor* and *display* interchangeably in most descriptions (and cover them interchangeably in Chapter 8). Technically, though, the two devices are different:

➡ **Monitor:** A *monitor* is a high-resolution television display based on a cathode ray tube (CRT). Because of the size of the CRT, it tends to be large and heavy. A modern PC can support two monitors to provide more workspace and to help you separate tasks (see **Figure 1-4**).

CRT monitor

Dual monitors provide more workspace.

Figure 1-4

A working monitor can be used with most computers. If you buy a new machine or need to replace a failed monitor, however, you'll probably have to switch to a display.

⟶ **Display:** A *display* (see **Figure 1-5**) uses a flat liquid crystal diode (LCD) system to show characters and graphics. Displays, which arrived with the first laptops, are thinner and lighter than monitors; use less electrical power; generate less heat; and may be sharper for tired eyes. The newest displays use light-emitting diodes (LED) instead of an LCD system.

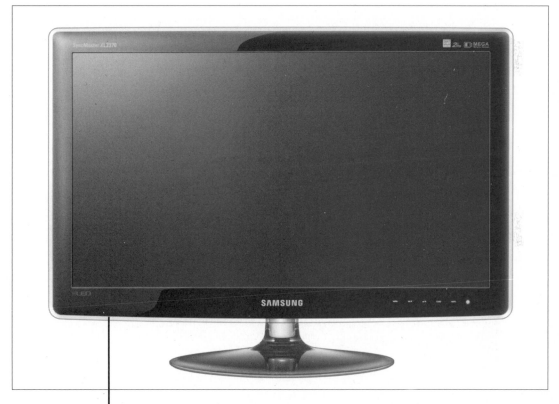

LCD and LED displays are thinner and lighter than CRT monitors.

Figure 1-5

 Given a choice, I'd get an LED display. LED displays are more expensive than LCD models, but they last longer, use less energy, and run a lot cooler.

Get the Picture (and Sound): Cameras, Speakers, and Microphones

➟ **Speakers:** Laptop computers generally have little speakers built into their cases; desktop machines offer connectors for external audio equipment. (For more information about these connectors, see "Connect the Parts: Ports and Hubs," later in this chapter.)

 To get the best sound from your computer, you should use speakers that have their own amplifier.

➟ **Microphone:** A computer's microphone (usually built in) allows you to chime in with your own narration or participate in online conference calls. For some users, a microphone can serve as a replacement for, or an enhancement to, a keyboard as a way to enter text and commands.

➟ **Video camera:** Video cameras for computers, called *Webcams*, are both small (some have a lens the size of the hole in a Cheerio) and inexpensive, so they're built into most laptops today. If you need to add an external Webcam to a desktop PC, you can buy one for $25 to $75. **Figure 1-6** shows a typical display-mounted Webcam from Logitech.

This 1.3 megapixel camera can mount on top of your display.

Figure 1-6

Go Online: Modems and Routers

➟ **Modem:** A *modem* (see **Figure 1-7**) is an essential
piece of hardware that allows your PC to communicate with the Internet or with other computers on a
local network. It can be either built-in or external.
The appearance, features, and speed of your modem
depend on what kind of service you use to connect

to the Internet or local network: dial-up or digital subscriber line (DSL) service from the phone company, or broadband cable from a cable television provider. You can find some maintenance and repair tips in Chapter 9.

Lights show connection status.

Figure 1-7

➠ **Router:** A *router* does what its name says: routes information from your computer across a network and out to the Internet. If you have only a single computer connected to the Internet, you don't need a router; you simply plug your computer directly into the modem. If you want to connect more than one computer to the Internet, however, you need a router to serve as a data traffic cop.

Routers come in many flavors. Some are stand-alone units; others are built into a wireless access point that lets your various computers connect wirelessly to the router and from there to the Internet. **Figure 1-8** shows a modern high-speed wireless router.

Wireless router

Figure 1-8

Put It on Paper: Printers

→ **Inkjet:** Inkjet printers use one or more cartridges filled with ink that literally spray images or text onto paper. Whether the printed information is text or photographs, it consists of tiny dots of ink placed very close together. The advantages of inkjet printers are size and cost — both small. (You can buy a serviceable inkjet printer for less than $50.) The disadvantages include relatively slow speed and high ink costs. A high-resolution color printer (the type you may use to print photographs) may use four or more ink cartridges, and depending on the amount of printing you do, the cost of maintaining an inkjet printer can be fairly high.

If you're willing to spend more for a high-end inkjet printer, you can get printing speeds of 20 pages per minute (or faster) for black and white and 10 to 30 seconds per page for color. In addition, you can get better picture quality than with a consumer-grade laser printer.

➠ **Laser:** Laser printers generally cost more than inkjet printers, but they can be faster, and operating costs are lower. A laser printer uses a laser beam to draw characters or images on an electrostatically charged drum, which attracts a very fine powder called toner and deposits the resulting image onto a piece of paper. Finally, the paper is passed through a hot fuser roller that melts the image onto the paper, making it permanent.

➠ **All-in-one:** For home or small-business use, consider an all-in-one printer (see **Figure 1-9**). These devices incorporate a fax machine, digital scanner, and (usually) inkjet printer in a single package. Prices are reasonable, and the device combination saves desk space. For the greatest flexibility, look for a unit that uses a sheet feeder so that you can scan a stack of pages or send multiple fax pages automatically.

Control panel lets you print with or without a computer

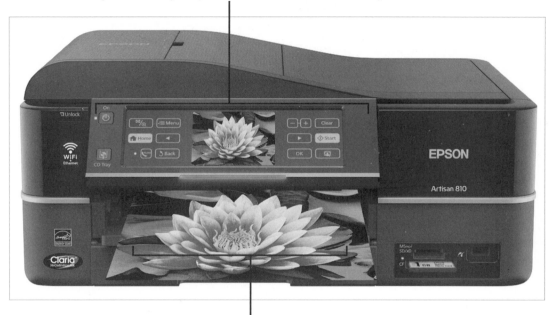

Scanner/copier tray

Figure 1-9

Connect the Parts: Ports and Hubs

⟶ **USB (Universal Serial Bus) ports:** These simple rectangular connectors (see **Figure 1-10**) are nearly ubiquitous on modern PCs and laptops because they can be used to link nearly any type of device. A computer may offer a bank of four or six ports, which look like tiny pizza ovens.

USB ports

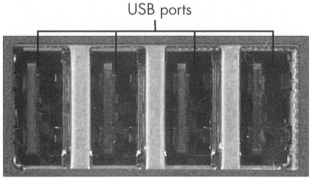

Figure 1-10

 The various versions of USB are downwardly compatible with older hardware, so a USB 2.0 port and cable should work with a device designed for USB 1.0, although they will exchange information at the slower speed of the older equipment. When USB 3.0 is available in late 2009 or 2010, it will work with devices designed for USB 1.0 and 2.0, at their original speeds.

➡ **Ethernet port:** An Ethernet cable plugged into this port attaches the computer to a local area network or high-speed modem. For more on this port, see Chapter 2.

➡ **Ethernet switch:** An Ethernet switch (see **Figure 1-11**) contains multiple Ethernet ports that connect multiple devices — computers, printers, wireless access points, and so on — to a network.

➡ **Hub:** Each USB port can connect directly to a single device or can be shared with multiple pieces of electronics by means of a *hub*, which is a bit like the power strip you may have behind your home entertainment system. A USB hub looks and functions much like an Ethernet switch. A cable plugged into a USB port on the PC connects it with the hub, which has two, four, or sometimes more connectors for USB cables.

Status lights show connections and network activity.

Ethernet ports attach devices to a network.

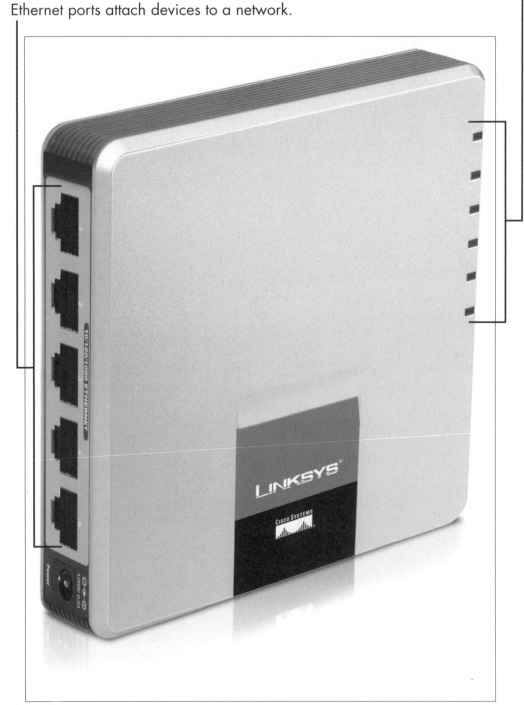

Figure 1-11

Protect Your PC: Surge Protectors and UPS Devices

➡ **Surge protector:** If a jolt of high voltage gets into your computer's motherboard (see Chapter 2), your computer is — to use the technical jargon — *fried.* That's why every computer (as well as any other expensive piece of electronic equipment in your home or office) should have a surge protector between its plug and the wall outlet. This device contains electrical components that can, in most circumstances, chop off any sudden spurts of high voltage.

In the worst situations, such as a lightning strike or a serious malfunction in an electrical line, a surge protector sacrifices itself like a bodyguard. Its internal parts melt to break the electrical circuit. With luck, this process happens so fast that the electrical surge won't get into the power supply or beyond.

➡ **Uninterruptible power supply (UPS):** If you want the highest level of protection from a power outage, consider adding a UPS device (see **Figure 1-12**) to your collection of equipment. This device is essentially a large battery with a bit of electronics to control its actions.

Your computer plugs into the UPS and draws its power from the battery; the UPS plugs into a wall socket, using the electrical current to keep topping off the battery. If the power goes off briefly or drops below ordinary levels momentarily, you should be able to keep on working without an interruption. In the case of an extended power outage, your computer should be able to use the battery long enough to allow you to save any open files and conduct an orderly shutdown.

Computer and other devices plug here

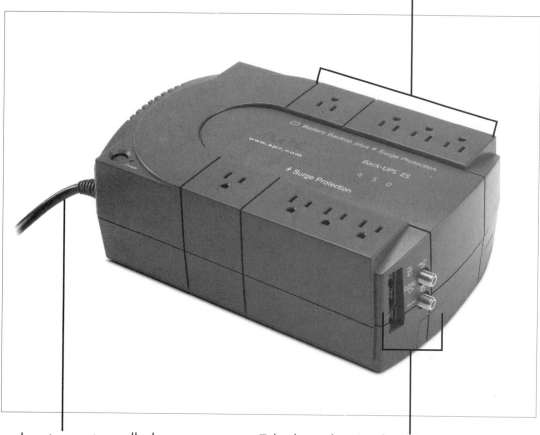

Input goes to wall plug

Telephone line and cable connect here

Figure 1-12

 Be sure to buy a UPS with a battery large enough to power your computer and its display for a reasonable period, such as 10 or 15 minutes.

Thinking Inside the Box

*B*efore you consider what's inside the box, think about the box itself: the case. It may lie on its side like a pizza box (this type is called a *desktop case)* or stand upright like a filing cabinet (and be known as a *tower case)*. Or you may be using a laptop or an integrated desktop machine. These configurations include the monitor with everything else and have unique shapes that depend on the manufacturers' whims.

However it stands, your case has four important assignments:

⮕ Holding together the internal components of the computer and creating a frame that allows the installation of certain features

⮕ Protecting electrical and other parts from damage by dirt, liquids, paper clips, and other threats

⮕ Working with the cooling fan to remove the heat that's generated by the electrical circuits and moving parts

⮕ Keeping radio-frequency radiation inside

Before you get nervous, let me assure you that you may never have to open the case of your desktop computer. In the case of a laptop computer, you probably wouldn't ever want to try, because it's not easy. This chapter just shows you what you would see if you were to perform a bit of exploratory surgery.

Assemble Your Toolkit

→ **Screwdrivers:** Most jobs require a single small Phillips-head (X-shaped) screwdriver; others call for a small and a medium-size flat-blade screwdriver.

 Some technicians prefer a ratchet-style driver that allows you to install or remove a screw by rotating your wrist; this design may reduce the chance that the screwdriver will slip out of the screw head. Also, a magnetized screwdriver helps you hold on to the screw while it's going into or coming out of the case.

 If you use a magnetized tool, avoid getting it close to your hard drive and other electronic components; they don't like magnets very much!

→ **Antistatic strap:** I recommend using an antistatic strap, similar to the one shown in **Figure 2-1**. You can buy one for a dollar or two, often from the same place where you buy computer parts. For details on using an antistatic strap, see "Get Grounded," later in this chapter.

→ **Stable work surface:** To do the job right, you need a sturdy, well-lighted workspace with enough elbow room for you and some additional space to hold any parts you remove.

→ **Writing materials, labels, and containers:** Put in place a notepad, a pencil or a plastic pen, and a set of numbered or marked containers (an empty egg carton works quite well).

Antistatic wrist strap

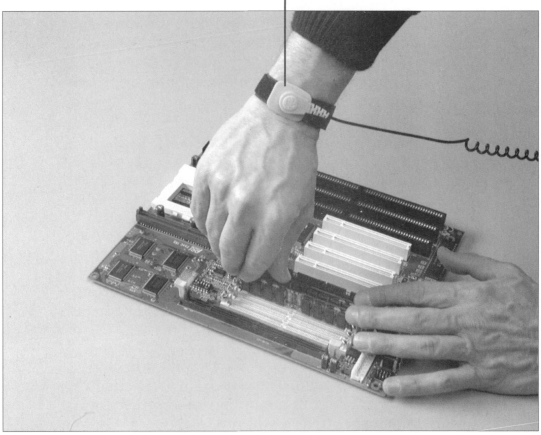

Figure 2-1

 You don't have to use a plastic pen, but when working around sensitive electronic equipment, it's always best to avoid the chance of shorting components with anything metal.

As you remove screws, clips, or cables, make notes about where particular screws used to reside and in which marked containers you placed them. Use the labels to identify all cables and connectors on your computer.

➠ **Camera:** Almost everyone has a digital or video camera. Put it to work by making a full set of images of the interior of your computer before you make any changes. If you run into trouble later while reinstalling parts or end up with an orphan screw, you should be able to figure out the solution by pressing Play on your camera.

Get Grounded

 Always use one of the techniques in this section to ground yourself before touching your computer's sensitive electronics; otherwise, you could create a damaging short. Here's what you absolutely *do not* want to do: Scuffle across a carpeted floor in your socks and then reach into the innards of your computer. That's one of the best ways to deliver a static shock that could blow the mind of your PC.

➠ **Use an antistatic strap.** Place the antistatic strap around one of your wrists. It usually interferes least if you put it on your nondominant arm (left arm for righties, right arm for lefties). Then connect the wire on the strap to a cold-water pipe, or tape it — metal to metal — to the center screw of a three-hole electrical outlet.

 Be careful not to put the wire in one of the holes meant for an electrical plug.

➠ **Use a desktop antistatic device.** You can install an antistatic device such as the touchpad shown in **Figure** 2-2, or buy a keyboard mat or antistatic touch strip.

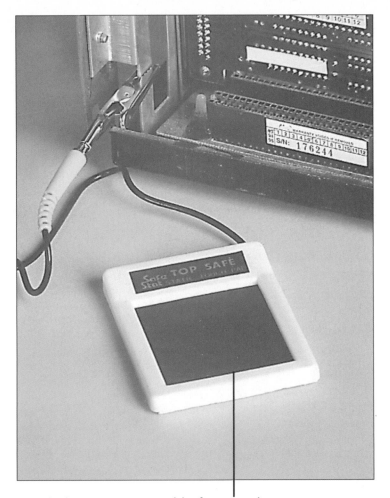

Touch this antistatic pad before touching your computer.
Figure 2-2

➠ **Discharge your body's static into a metal object.** If
you don't use an antistatic strap or device, position
your chair close to a cold-water pipe or the center
screw of an electrical outlet; when you're seated and
ready to begin work, touch the pipe or screw to discharge your body's static electricity into it. If you
can't do that, seat yourself, touch something metal
and substantial, and then stay where you are without
moving around.

In most cases, simply touching the outside of the computer case before you touch any of the internal components is enough to bring your body to the same electrical potential as the component you'll touch next.

Open the Computer's Case

 PCs come in dozens of designs, so spending a few moments studying the instruction manual first may be helpful.

1. Place your computer on the work surface, with your tools, writing materials, and parts containers at hand.

2. Unplug the computer's power cord, and label and remove all other cables and power connectors.

3. Ground yourself (see "Get Grounded," earlier in this chapter).

4. Open the case.

- **Clamshell case:** If your computer's case is a clamshell design, it opens like a book when you release one or two latches or clips; no tools are required (see **Figure** 2-3).

- **Upright tower case:** Lay it on its side so that the motherboard is face up and parallel with your working surface. Then remove the connecting screws or clips, placing them in one of the labeled containers on your work surface.

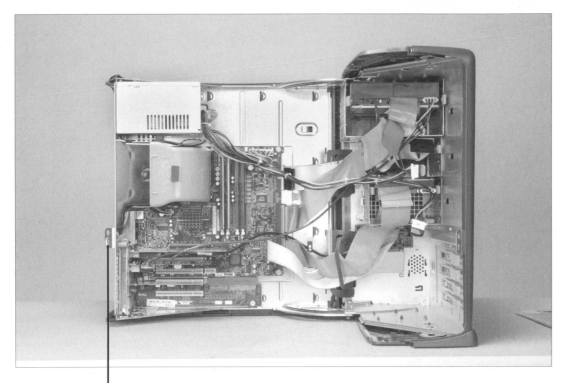

Release latch

Figure 2-3

 You'll have to inspect your computer case to determine how to orient it. Most cases are built as a box with a top that's removable when the computer is on its side, so put the deep side down and remove the plate on top. If your case has two removable sides, the proper orientation *probably* is with the power supply down on the work surface. (The power supply is behind the fan opening on the rear of the case; also see Step 5.)

5. With the cover removed, examine the inside of the computer (see **Figure 2-4**). You should be able to spot three major components easily:

Microprocessor   Power supply

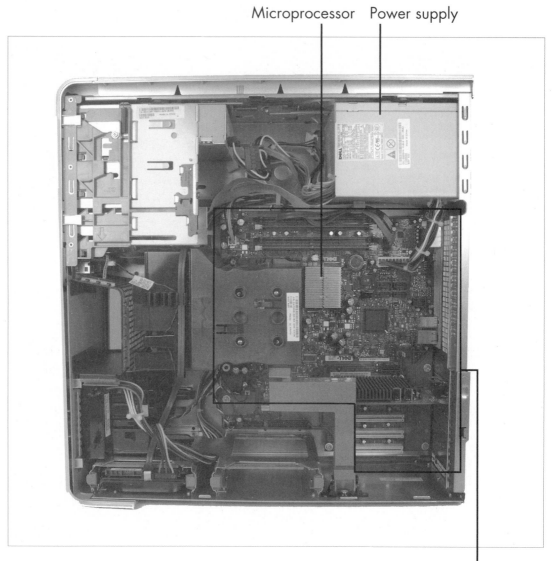

Motherboard

Figure 2-4

- **Power supply:** A sealed metal case holds the power supply. On the outside of the case is the incoming connector for the AC cord, and within the case is a thicket of cables (usually black, white, red, and yellow) and connectors. For more on the power supply, see "Tour the Computer's Infrastructure," later in this chapter.

- **Microprocessor:** The microprocessor is easy to locate because of a fan, heat sink, or sometimes a plastic tunnel intended to move cooling air over its top and out a vent. I describe it in more detail in the next section.

- **Motherboard:** The flat motherboard (see the next section for more info) holds dozens of chips and connectors, including a set of long slots for upright memory modules. Most motherboards have two or four such slots, which are usually black with a set of plastic lockdown/ejector clips at each end. In **Figure** 2-5, slots 2 and 4 have memory installed, latched in place with clips; slots 1 and 3 show memory modules partially inserted.

Installed memory modules.

Partly installed memory modules.

Figure 2-5

Find Out What Makes Your Computer Think

➡ **Motherboard:** In a modern PC, the motherboard has two principal purposes:

- Providing electrical and communication wiring to sockets that hold the central processing unit (CPU) and chipset

- Managing the *bus* — a device that connects the computer's brain to its memory, storage devices, and input/output ports

➡ **Microprocessor:** Sometimes called the CPU or just the processor, this chip is the brain of the computer. Within this small chip are hundreds of millions of tiny circuits that switch on or off to move or manipulate bits of data. In modern PCs, most microprocessors are made by Intel or AMD. **Figure 2-6** shows an Intel Core 2 Quad microprocessor.

 Although it's theoretically possible to take out the microprocessor in your computer and replace it with a faster or more capable unit, you may find that the new brain won't match the personality (see the next paragraph). Also, this transplant may not make economic sense.

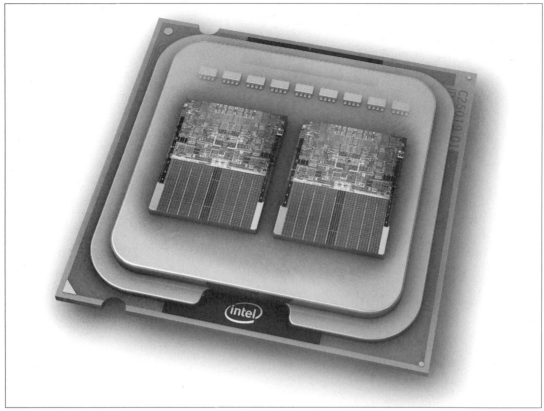

Figure 2-6

➟ **Chipset:** If the microprocessor is the computer's brain, the chipset is its personality. The specialized chips hold instructions that manage the computer's ability to (among other things) draw graphics onscreen; play music through speakers; and react to input from the keyboard, mouse, or other device. **Figure 2-7** shows an Intel chipset below a Pentium microprocessor.

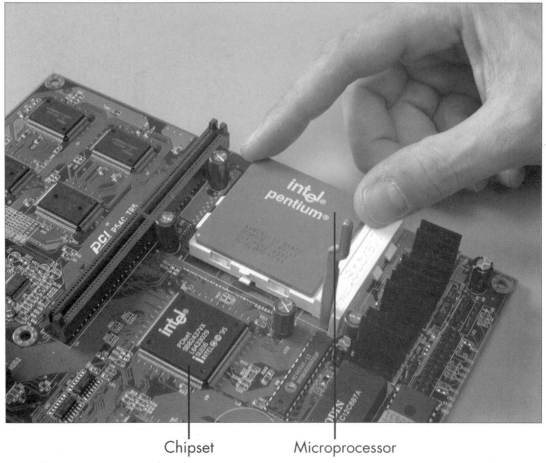

Chipset   Microprocessor

Figure 2-7

See Where Your Computer Stores Your Stuff

➠ **Hard drive:** A computer's hard drive is essentially a very
fancy record player. It may have more than one platter
(think of platters as records — see **Figure 2-8**), and it
can work with data recorded on either side and on
more than one platter. Hard drives are inside a sealed
case because the read/write head (also shown in Figure
2-8) floats or flies like an airplane wing just a few thou-
sandths of an inch above the rotating disk within. The
tiniest piece of dust or bagel crumb would look like an
iceberg in the path of the *Titanic,* and the result would
be similar: a disastrous loss of computer life.

Platters   Read/write head

Figure 2-8

⟶ **Optical disk drive (CD or DVD):** Optical drives can come in three designs:

- **Read:** Like the CD player you may have in your car or a DVD player in the rec room, this type of device can only play back the contents of the disc.

- **Read/write:** A read/write drive, often referred to as a CD-R or DVD-R drive, can play back a disc and also burn data to a recordable blank disc for later retrieval and use.

- **Read/write/rewritable:** This type of drive, called a CD-RW or DVD-RW drive, can play back, write, erase, and rewrite data on the disc.

Figure 2-9 shows a typical internal optical drive.

Drive

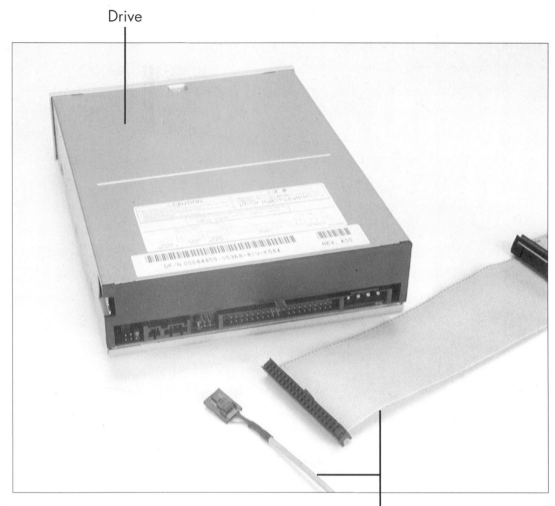

Data and audio cables

Figure 2-9

➠ **Flash memory:** Flash memory uses external devices called USB flash drives, memory sticks, memory cards, or memory keys (similar to the one shown in **Figure 2-10**) to store information. I use flash memory devices to transfer files between computers that aren't connected and also to make temporary backups of files. Flash memory is also used in digital cameras, cellphones, and portable music players.

Flash memory key   Case

Figure 2-10

Tour the Computer's Infrastructure

➟ **Power supply:** An essential part of any desktop PC is the power supply (see **Figure 2-11**), which converts electricity coming from a wall outlet from AC (alternating current) to DC (direct current) and reduces the voltage from 120 or 240 volts (depending on where you live or work) to the smaller requirements of your machine. Under the case of your PC, the power supply usually sits in its own sealed gray or black metal box. Wall current comes in through a cord and goes out of the power supply in a series of colored wires that connect to the motherboard, memory, storage, and other devices.

➟ **Cooling system:** A computer's cooling (or thermal energy dissipation) system may be easier to understand if you just call it the fan. The processor inside the computer, its memory, and the motors that spin the hard drive and optical drive all produce heat, which can damage components, so designers have to dump the heat to the outside.

Figure 2-11

Most modern PCs have an intake hole on the front of the case and an exhaust port on the back, with one or more fans that draw air through the system to flow over the hot spots. Mazelike baffles at the entrances and exits allow air to pass through but block radio-frequency radiation from escaping. Your computer may have only one fan that's integrated into the power supply, or it may have multiple fans inside the case. **Figure** 2-12 shows a cooling fan for a Pentium microprocessor.

Clip-on cooling fan

Figure 2-12

Never place a computer flat against a wall or other solid object that would block the air ports and cause the machine to overheat. Every few months, use a vacuum to clear dust out of the air intakes and exits.

➠ **External ports:** Just like their maritime counterparts, computer ports are designed for coming and going traffic. Think of them as doorways for data. A typical set of external ports, shown in **Figure 2-13**, provides links to a keyboard and mouse, to external USB devices (such as a hard drive or flash memory key), and to an Ethernet network.

On older desktop computers, the back or side panels are jammed with rows of specialized connectors (for a monitor, keyboard, mouse, and so on) and several multipurpose ports for things like modems, printers, scanners, and external storage. Today's PCs dispense with most of these ports, using advanced multipurpose connectors. Most modern computers can connect to just about anything through a set of USB ports.

➠ **Internal ports:** Inside the case, you'll find ports on the motherboard that connect to the external ports or attach the internal hard drive to the motherboard.

Figure 2-13

Looking Through Windows and Other Software

Computers have two major types of components: hardware and software. I discuss the hardware side in Chapter 2. In this chapter, I cover basic software that can help you understand how your computer operates and fix some things that may go wrong.

Windows includes several applications that you'll probably use regularly to manage your PC and fix operational issues. You find many of these applications in *Control Panel*, a window on the innards of your computer where you can twiddle with the dials and throw a few switches *while the machine is running.* No screwdrivers or pliers are required.

You'll also want (and need) several third-party software packages to help you with everything from office work such as word processing and spreadsheet design to scanning, photography, and other tasks that you'll want to perform as you find out more about your computer.

Tour Windows

1. Choose Start⇨All Programs⇨Accessories.

2. Choose the appropriate command for your version of Windows:

- **Windows XP:** Tour Windows XP

- **Vista:** Welcome Center (see **Figure 3-1**)

- **Windows 7:** Getting Started

Click a topic to launch a description or connect to the internet to get more information.

Figure 3-1

3. In Windows XP, choose whether you want an animated display with sound or a nonanimated tour. (Vista and Windows 7 skip this screen and go straight to the one shown in Figure 3-1.)

4. Choose Go Online to Learn More (Windows 7) or What's New in Windows (Vista) to visit a Microsoft help site that provides videos and other information about your version of the operating system.

 You can go directly to the help site from Internet Explorer. For Vista, go to `http://windowshelp.microsoft.com/windows`. For Windows 7, go to `www.windows.microsoft.com`.

Open Control Panel

1. Choose Start⇨Control Panel or My Computer⇨Control Panel to open the Control Panel window.

2. Choose a different view, if you want, by clicking the Classic View or Category View option on the left side of the window (see **Figure 3-2**). In Classic View, the Control Panel applications are listed in alphabetical order.

3. Study the Control Panel window to familiarize yourself with the applications that you can access here.

Click this option to switch to Category View   Classic view in Windows XP

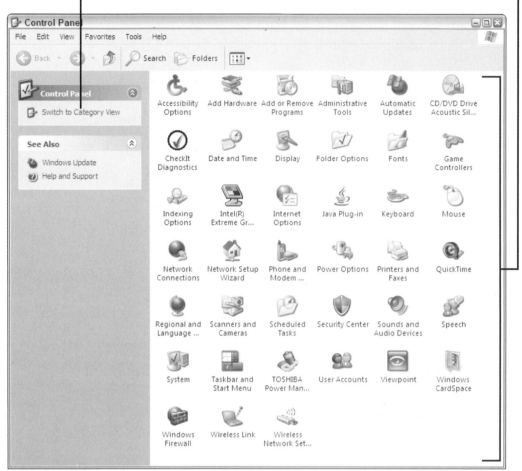

Figure 3-2

Customize Your Display

1. From Control Panel double-click the Display icon to launch the Display Properties utility (XP), or choose Personalization from the Appearance and Personalization menu in Windows 7 or Vista.

To go directly to the Display Properties dialog without going through the Control Panel, right-click anywhere on the Windows Desktop and choose Properties (XP), or right-click the Desktop and choose Personalize (Vista and Windows 7).

2. Select a general area to view or change from the tabs at the top of the Display Properties dialog (XP) or choose an area for modification from the menu choices at the left of the screen (Vista and Windows 7). For example, you can choose a new desktop background from the images installed with Windows or use your own art or photograph (the Desktop tab in XP, or the Personalization screen in Vista and Windows 7). You can do the same with the screen saver (Windows screen savers or your own images).

 Vista and Windows 7 handle these display settings significantly differently from Windows XP, but the basic concept is the same. Instead of a tabbed display, Vista gives you menu choices in the Personalization display, which you will find under Appearance and Personalization in the Category view. Windows 7 uses the Personalization dialog as well, but in Windows 7 you set desktop themes, screen saver settings, sounds. and desktop background, all at once.

3. Click Apply to preview your changes (XP). In Vista and Windows 7 the display changes immediately when you make the choice. See **Figure** 3-3.

4. Make additional modifications as desired, then click OK to accept the changes and close the Display Properties dialog (XP) or just close the Personalization dialog in Vista and Windows 7. For more information managing and repairing your monitor and display settings, see Chapter 8.

Click Apply to preview

Figure 3-3

Set Internet Options

1. From Control Panel, double-click the Internet Options dialog. This choice will be in the Vista and Windows 7 Network and Internet Category. **Figure 3-4** shows the Programs tab from the Vista Internet Options dialog.

2. Click the Programs tab to set a variety of program options for Internet access. You can choose the programs you want to use from the pull-down lists at each data entry field on this dialog.

3. Click the Connections tab to tell Windows how you want to reach the Internet. Click Setup on this dialog to launch a Connections Wizard to help you establish an Internet connection.

Click the tab to choose the options
you want to view or change.

Click OK or Apply to accept the changes.
Figure 3-4

 The Internet Options dialog box is available on the
Tools menu of Internet Explorer.

4. Study the choices on the Advanced menu to make your
Internet experience be just what you want it to be. Here's
where you set security options, specify some Explorer display options, set printing options and more.

Configure Mail

1. From Control Panel double click the Mail icon to display
the Mail Setup dialog. **Figure 3-5** shows the Vista Mail
Setup dialog.

Click E-Mail Accounts to set up a new account
or modify one you've already established.

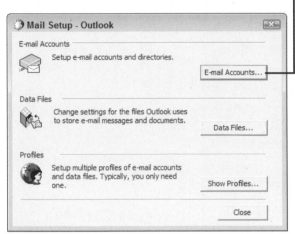

Figure 3-5

 Windows 7 does not include an intrinsic E-Mail
client like Outlook Express, which comes with XP.
You'll need to download and configure the new
Windows Live Mail client, a free Windows 7 upgrade.
An earlier version of this client, called simply
Windows Mail, is built into Vista. See Download and
Configure Windows Live Applications later in this
chapter for more information.

2. For the most part you can ignore the Data Files and
Profiles options on this dialog. The default settings will
handle all your needs.

3. Click E-mail Accounts to add a new E-mail account or
view or change an existing account. If you have previously configured an e-mail account, you will see a dialog
that shows that account and lets you modify it or add a
new one. If this is your first e-mail account, Windows
will step you through several dialog screens to input the
information required to make the account work.

You'll need several pieces of key information to properly add or reconfigure an e-mail account. Information from your Internet Service Provider (ISP) will answer these: Account Type (IMAP or POP3), IMAP or POP3 server, SMTP Server, your e-mail address (xxx@yyy.zzz), your username (how you log into the e-mail server), and your password.

4. Click Finish on the final dialog to accept changes or create the new e-mail account.

 On the e-mail settings screen where you enter the core information for your account, you can click Test Account Settings to make sure your settings are correct before you actually create the account.

Use the Network Setup Wizard

1. From Control Panel double-click the Network Setup Wizard icon (XP and Vista) to launch the wizard. The Vista setup dialog is shown in **Figure 3-6.** In Windows 7 open the Network and Sharing center from the Icon view, or choose Network Status and Tasks in the category view, then click on Set up a New Connection or Network.

 In Vista and Windows 7, this one Control Panel choice lets you configure your local area network and also set up an Internet connection. In Windows XP the Network Setup Wizard gets you to the Internet. To create a new Local Area Network connection, choose Network Connections from the Control Panel, and Wireless Network Setup to configure a wireless network.

2. Click Connect to a Network on the Set up a wireless router or access point screen to add your computer to an existing network.

Click what do I need . . . to learn more about networking.

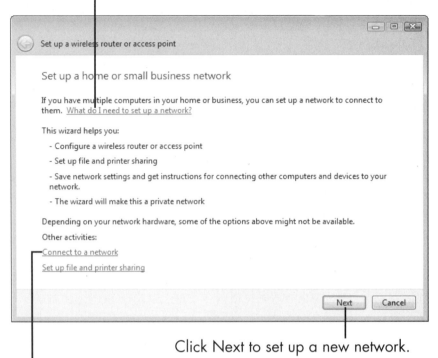

Click Next to set up a new network.

Click Connect to a Network if you're
adding a computer to an existing network.

Figure 3-6

3. Click Next at the bottom of this dialog to set up a new
network. Windows will scan for wireless access points
and step you through configuring them for your network.

Configure Printers and Faxes

1. From Control Panel, double-click the Printers and Faxes
icon (XP). In Vista and Windows 7 choose Devices and
Printers to view a list with icons of printers and fax devices.

2. Click Add a Printer to add a new device to your computer. **Figure 3-7** shows the initial Add a Printer dialog in
Vista and Windows 7. Windows XP displays a wizard
welcome screen, then lets you choose the type of printer
to install on the second dialog.

Choose Local or Network (remote) printer.

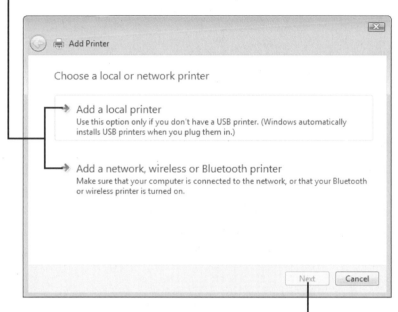

Click Next to let the wizard help you finish the installation.

Figure 3-7

3. Choose Local or Network printer from the wizard dialog and click Next to move to the next screen. You will see different screens after this, depending on what type of printer you are installing. Windows will try to find a printer to install automatically, but you may be asked for printer manufacturer, model, network address (for a remote printer), and other information.

If you are installing a printer attached to a networked computer or other network device (such as a wireless access point or router), choose the printer host device from the port list on the next printer wizard dialog. For a stand-alone Ethernet connected printer you may need to create a new TCP/IP.

4. Follow the wizard to the next to last page, answering the questions as you go, and choose Yes to print a test page. This will verify your settings before you finish the installation.

5. On the last screen click Finish to complete the installation.

Explore Windows Accessories

1. Choose Start⇨All Programs⇨Accessories. **Figure** 3-8 shows the accessories list from Windows 7. Vista and XP will have slightly different applications in this list. As with the Control Panel, study this list to familiarize yourself with the types of utilities here.

Some entries are applications; others are folders with additional programs.

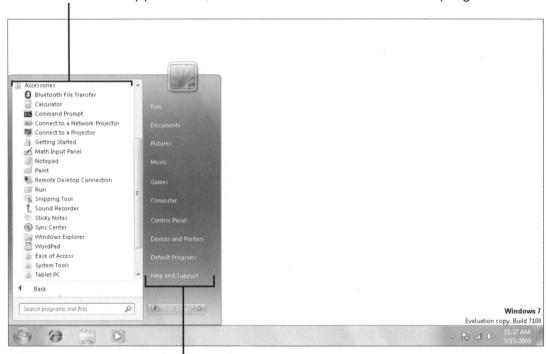

Hover your mouse pointer over an entry for more information.

Figure 3-8

Vista and Windows 7 display drop-down menus when you choose Accessories or one of the Accessories submenus. Windows XP display successive menus as you hover your mouse over each parent menu.

2. To use one of the Accessories applications, simply click the menu item you want to use.

3. To exit the Accessories menu, move your mouse pointer outside the menu area and click on the desktop.

Use Windows Explorer

1. Choose Start⇨All Programs⇨Accessories.

2. Click Windows Explorer to open this utility. **Figure** 3-9 shows the Vista Explorer utility.

This is a utility you will use frequently. From the Accessories program list you can right-drag the Windows Explorer icon to your desk to create a shortcut to make access easier.

3. Click the right-facing triangle to the left of a folder name in the Folders display at the left of the screen to present a list of the sub-folders within.

4. Click a folder name to display its contents on the right side of the Explorer screen.

You can move files easily among directories. First display the folder contents for the source location of a file or files, then click the triangle to the left of a main folder on the left to display the destination. Drag the file from the right window display across to the folder name to move it to the new location.

Click a folder name on the left of the screen to display its contents on the right. Note the additional menu items.

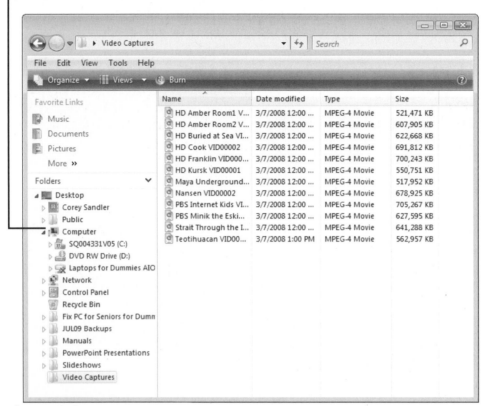

Figure 3-9

5. Click in the Search field at the upper right of the Explorer window and type all or a part of a file name to find it. Narrow the search by first selecting a folder at the left. If you select Computer (Vista and Windows 7) the search routine will look in all of your storage devices for the specified file. In Windows XP click on the Search spyglass on the Explorer toolbar and fill out the information displayed on the next screen.

6. If you have additional computers or storage devices on your network, Windows will find them and show them in the Network list on the left of the screen. If you have shared resources on these devices, you can access them from Explorer.

7. Click the back and forward arrows at the upper left of the display to step through locations you have browsed since you opened Windows Explorer.

View System Information

1. Choose Start➪All Programs➪Accessories.

2. Select System Tools.

3. Select System Information. The System Information utility generates a complete report on what's in your computer, similar to the one shown in **Figure 3-10**. You can refer to this system information at any time to make sure that you have the latest system updates, as well as to determine whether your system meets new applications' criteria for memory, hard drive space, and the like.

 Here's a shortcut to system information: Open the Start menu, right-click Computer or My Computer (Windows XP), and choose Properties from the shortcut menu.

Choose Hardware, Applications, or another topic to drill down into system information.

Note your Windows version, system memory, and other key features of your computer.

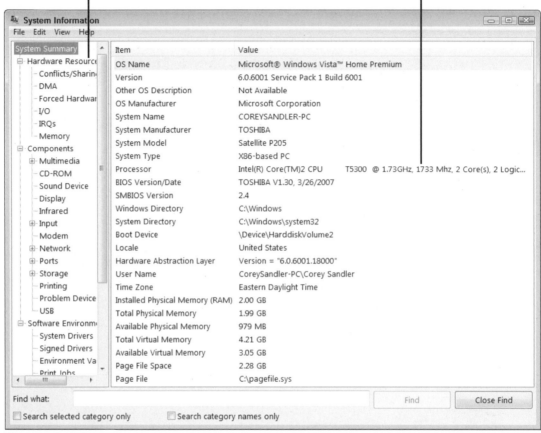

Figure 3-10

Run the Program Compatibility Wizard

If anything can go wrong, it will, so you need to know about this utility, which can help you resolve application problems (see **Figure 3-11**).

1. Choose the appropriate command for your operating system:

- **Windows XP:** Choose Start➪All Programs➪ Accessories; then choose Program Compatibility Wizard.

- **Vista:** Open Control Panel; choose Programs, and select Use an Older Program with This Version of Windows.

- **Windows 7:** Open the Control Panel, choose Programs, and select Run Programs Made for Previous Versions of Windows.

Click Next from this opening screen to launch the wizard.

Figure 3-11

2. Click Next to launch the Program Compatibility wizard. What happens next depends on your operating system. Windows XP will ask whether you want to search for program problems, use a program on a CD-ROM, or locate a program manually; Vista and Windows 7 simply search your hard drive for applications and display a list of those applications.

3. (Windows XP only) Select the program you want to test, and click Next.

4. Again, what happens at this point depends on your operating system. Windows XP asks which Windows version, if any, you want to test the program against. Vista and Windows 7 let you choose to test the program or tell the wizard what problems you have experienced.

5. After Windows checks the program and prompts you to do so, launch the program. If the program runs properly, you can close the wizard. If not, you have an opportunity to try new settings.

Part II

Keeping Your PC Healthy with Preventive Maintenance

The 5th Wave   By Rich Tennant

"I couldn't get this 'job skills' program to work on my PC, so I replaced the motherboard, upgraded the BIOS and wrote a program that links it to my personal database. It told me I wasn't technically inclined and should pursue a career in sales."

Taking Care of Software

You have a choice: Leave your operating system and programs untouched, or subject them to regular updates. In theory, you *might* be safe never updating Windows if

- → You never add software.

- → You never make any hardware changes, using your PC in the same condition in which it was delivered from the factory.

- → You never connect to the Internet or to any other computer over a local area network.

- → You never accept a file from another user on a CD, DVD, or other device.

If you have that sort of hermetically sealed machine, though, you're missing out on much of the fun and productivity that come from making connections. What's more, your PC's operating system and its software programs may fall behind the times. Without updates, you won't benefit from improvements, bug fixes, and new defenses against virus and malware attacks.

Sometimes, you also need to update or even replace *device drivers* — small collections of programming code that interpret commands between Windows and devices inside or outside the PC. Drivers sometimes get damaged by things such as electrical spikes, hard disk problems, or computer viruses.

In this chapter, I show you how to care for Windows and other software.

Check for Windows Updates Manually

1. Choose Start⇨Control Panel, and look for the Windows Update icon in the far-left column of the Control Panel window. (In Vista, you see the words "Check for updates." In 7, you must choose the icon view first.) It appears there in both Classic View, which displays all the available major utilities as separate icons, and Category View, which groups icons of similar types. (See Chapter 3 for more information about Control Panel's views.)

2. What you do next depends on your version of Windows:

- **Windows XP:** Double-click Windows Update.

- **Vista:** Click Check for Updates (see **Figure 4-1**).

- **Windows 7:** If you're viewing Control Panel in Classic View, click the Windows Update icon. If you're in Classic View, click System and Security; then click Windows Update in the resulting list.

Whichever method you use, a Microsoft Update Web page appears when system updates are available for your computer.

 Different versions of Windows present slightly different update pages. In general, however, the update software goes directly to the Internet, checks for updates to your system, and then tells you whether updates are available.

Update link in Windows Vista's Control Panel

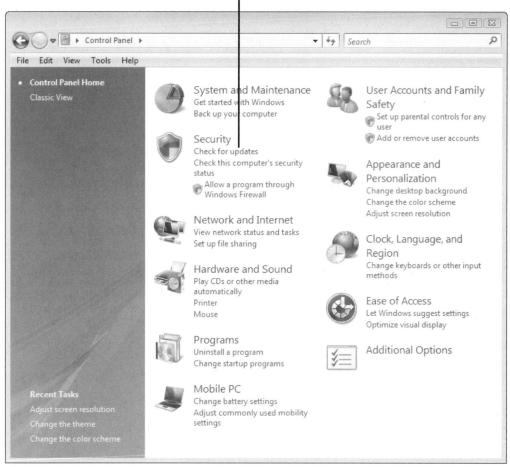

Figure 4-1

3. In the update Web page, choose the Express or Custom option to install available updates.

4. Click the Install Updates button (see **Figure 4-2**) to download and install the updates on your PC, or click the View Available Updates link to get more information about them first.

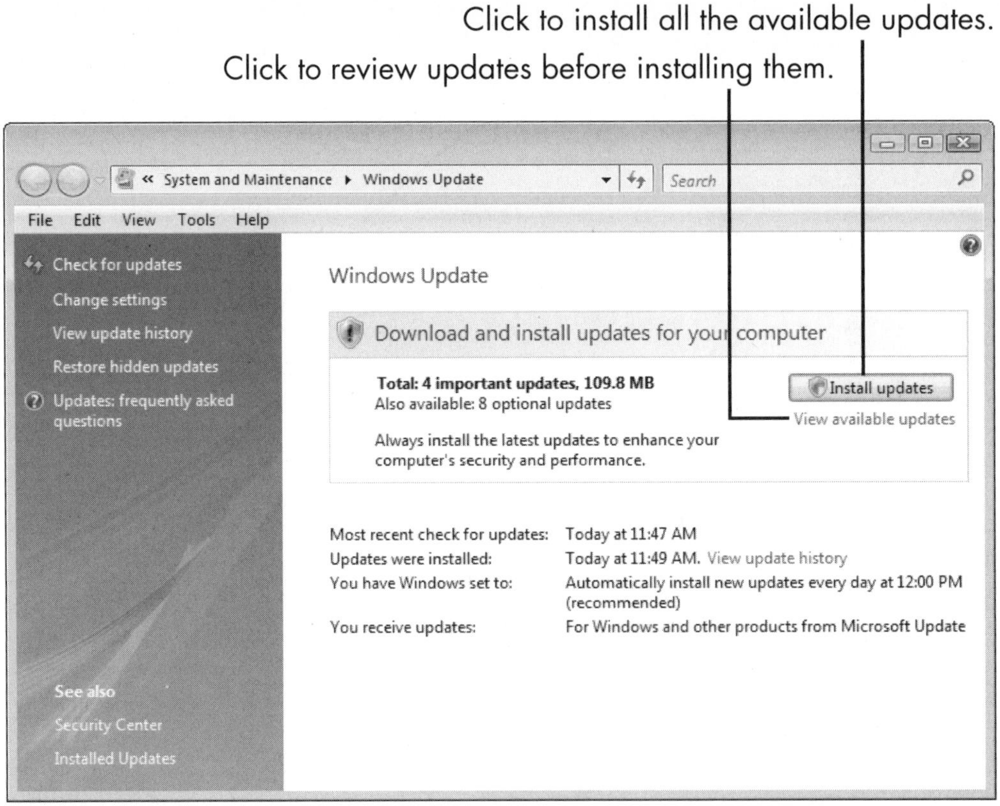

Click to install all the available updates.

Click to review updates before installing them.

Figure 4-2

Check for Windows Updates Automatically

1. Choose Start⇨Control Panel to open the Control Panel window.

2. Double-click the Automatic Updates icon (see **Figure** 4-3).

3. Choose one of the available options:

- **Automatic Updates:** Microsoft recommends this option, which is marked by a friendly green shield with a checkmark. If you select this option, you can set your computer to communicate with the Microsoft mothership automatically on a particular day of the week or every day, as well as tell it what time of day to look for updates.

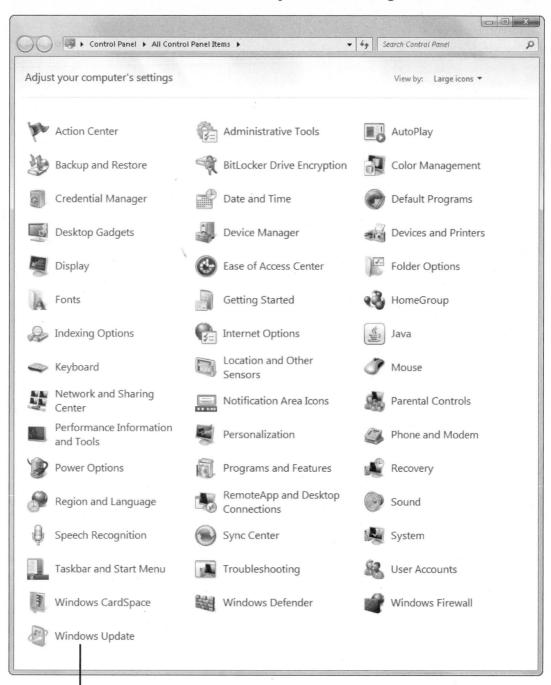

Automatic updates icon

Figure 4-3

Most users should select this option. I suggest that you schedule daily checks for updates at a time when you're least likely to be interrupted.

- **Download Updates for Me, but Let Me Choose When to Install Them:** This option allows you to look at the list of suggested updates that Microsoft sends your way and accept or reject them individually.

Remember to check the notification icon in the notification area of the Windows desktop and initiate putting any new software in place. If you don't, the updates will be on your computer but won't be installed in Windows.

- **Notify Me but Don't Automatically Download or Install Them:** If you choose this option, Microsoft sends the updates that it thinks your computer needs. Read the list, choose the updates you want, and then initiate installation.

- **Turn Off Automatic Updates:** This option is decorated with a red shield filled with an X as a warning. Microsoft advises that your computer will be vulnerable unless you install updates regularly. When Automatic Updates is off, it's up to you to visit Windows Update on your own (see "Check for Windows Updates Manually," earlier in this chapter). This option is not recommended for general use.

About once or twice in each operating system's life cycle, Microsoft offers a major package of updates and revisions called a *Service Pack*, which is about as close to a completely new version of Windows as you can get. I cover checking for and installing Service Pack updates later in this chapter.

Update Other Software

1. If you haven't already, register all of your applications with their manufacturers. It's best to do this when you first install the software on your computer.

2. Choose your update preference:

- **Automatic:** Some third-party programs offer regular automatic updates that last until a new version of the program is released or for a specific period. Antivirus and Internet security programs, for example, typically come set up to receive updates that are sent on a regular schedule or whenever new threats are discovered. You may see an update notice in your taskbar.

- **Manual:** If you decide not to get automatic updates or don't have that option, train yourself to get on a regular schedule of checking to see whether updates are being offered. While your PC is connected to the Internet, click the program's "check for updates" link (usually in a Help menu) to go online and check for available updates, as shown in **Figure** 4-4. Then follow the onscreen instructions.

Nearly all software manufacturers assume that users have access to high-speed Internet connections, so they deliver updates online. A few companies offer to ship a CD or DVD with updates (and may charge you for that special service).

3. Install any required updates. In addition to fixing bugs, required updates may add compatibility with new file formats or keep the software in step with changes in Windows.

In McAfee, click this link to check for updates manually.

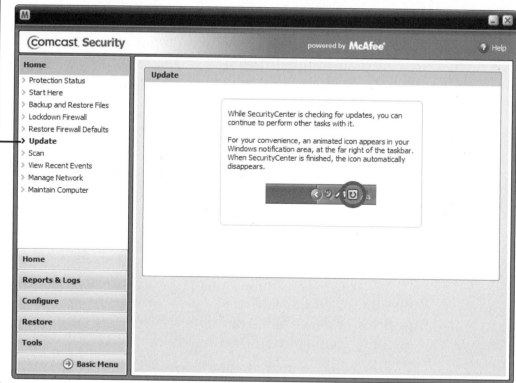

Figure 4-4

4. Decide whether to install optional updates, which are . . . well, optional. They may address minor issues that may not apply to your system or to the tasks you perform, or they may add some functions that you don't need or want. Read the updates' descriptions as well as system requirements, and make your own decision about whether to put them on your computer.

Check Your Service Pack Status

1. Choose Start➪Run to open the Run dialog box. In Vista and Windows 7 type it into the search box.

2. Type **winver** and then click OK.

The resulting dialog box shows what version of Windows you're running and which Service Pack is installed.

 Cautious users, including me, usually put off installing a Service Pack for a few weeks after it's released to the public; I prefer to allow other people to try it first and look for any major incompatibilities. To take this course, you'll have to conduct manual updates (see "Check for Windows Updates Manually," earlier in this chapter), because Windows will install Service Packs for you automatically as part of the update process.

Check for and Install Service Pack Updates

1. Open Internet Explorer.

2. Go to **http://update.microsoft.com.**

3. Click Express (Recommended).

If you don't have the latest Service Pack installed, Windows will display a dialog box similar to the one shown in **Figure 4-5**.

 If you haven't updated Windows in a while, you may have additional software to install before you can install the Service Pack. Follow any onscreen instructions.

4. Close all running programs.

5. Click the Install button to start the installation.

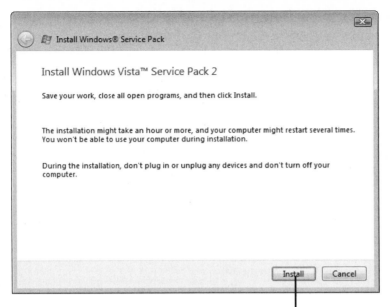

Click Install when you're ready to download the latest Server Pack.

Figure 4-5

Download and Configure Windows Live Applications

I have some bad news and I have some good news. Don't worry, the good news is better than the bad news. The bad news is, Windows 7 doesn't come with some of the neat and useful applications you've come to expect from earlier versions of Windows. No E-Mail client, for example, and no video editing and photo management applications.

Bummer.

But the good news is, Microsoft's new concept (Windows Live) offers all these and more as free downloads. You just have to go online and install them. And the better news is, these new versions of old favorites have some significant enhancements, so you'll like them even better.

1. Open Internet Explorer and type http://download. live.com in the browser address bar. The Windows Live download page appears (see **Figure 4-6**).

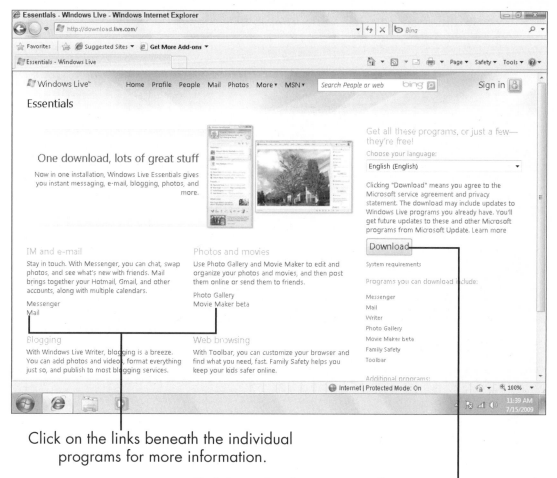

Click on the links beneath the individual
programs for more information.

Click Download to retrieve all Live programs at once.

Figure 4-6

2. Click Download to open a Download dialog.

3. Click Run if you are asked if you want to Run or Save the program.

4. Depending on your security settings, you may be asked if it is OK for the downloaded program to make changes to your computer. Say Yes. The Windows Live installer will launch and display the screen shown in **Figure** 4-7.

Check the programs you want to install.

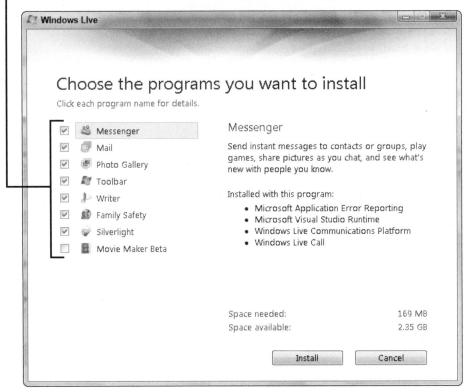

Figure 4-7

 Click each program name to display a short description to help you decide whether you want to install it.

5. Click Install. You may be asked to close open programs so the installer can make changes to them.

6. Click Continue after the download and initial install are complete to set some configuration options.

7. Click Sign Up if you want to create a Windows Live online ID at this time. If not click Close.

8. Choose Start⇨All Programs and click Windows Live to display a list of the programs you just installed.

9. Click a program name to launch the application.

Fix Corrupted Program Files

It may be a dirty little secret among computer users, but your program files and other data can become corrupted and dysfunctional through no direct fault of your own. If you practice good hardware mainte-nance and back up your working hard drives regularly, the chance of suffering corrupted files is small. Fortunately, if your files *do* become corrupted (and they probably will, if you use your computer long enough), you have a way to recover.

1. Close the offending program, if it's running.

2. Choose Start⇨Control Panel to open the Control Panel window.

3. Follow the instructions in "Uninstall a Misbehaving Program When All Else Fails," later in this chapter. You'll be asked to choose the program from a list.

Fix Corrupted Device Drivers

1. Choose Start⇨Control Panel to open the Control Panel window.

2. Follow the appropriate step for your version of Windows:

- **Windows XP:** Double-click the System icon; then click the Hardware tab in the resulting dialog box, and choose Device Manager.

- **Vista and Windows 7:** Click System and Security (in Windows 7) or System and Maintenance (in Vista); then choose System⇨Device Manager.

Whichever method you use, the Device Manager dialog box opens.

3. Select the troublesome hardware device.

4. Click the Driver tab (see **Figure** 4-8).

Click to launch the Windows update wizard.

Figure 4-8

5. Click the Update Driver button.

6. Follow the onscreen instructions to help Windows find a driver for the selected hardware. You may be asked to use the installation CD or DVD that came with your hardware. If you have it, use it; if you don't, Windows will go online to search the Internet for the proper driver.

You probably can update the driver yourself, direct from the source. Go to the manufacturer's support Web page and enter the model of your hardware, and you're likely to be able to download a self-installing driver. When you take this approach, you may get additional software, such as (in the case of a camera or scanner) a photo-editing application.

Uninstall a Misbehaving Program When All Else Fails

You have three ways to remove a program from a computer running Windows. The first two methods usually work well; the third is dangerous and not recommended.

➥ **Windows utility:** Use the Add or Remove Programs utility (Windows XP) or the Uninstall or Change a Program utility (Vista and Windows 7).

 Not all programs that you install on your computer make use of this utility.

1. Choose Start⇨Control Panel to open the Control Panel window.

2. Follow the appropriate step for your version of Windows:

- **Windows XP:** Double-click the Add or Remove Programs icon to open the Add or Remove Programs window.

- **Vista and Windows 7:** Click the Programs and Features icon to open the Programs and Features window (see **Figure 4-9**).

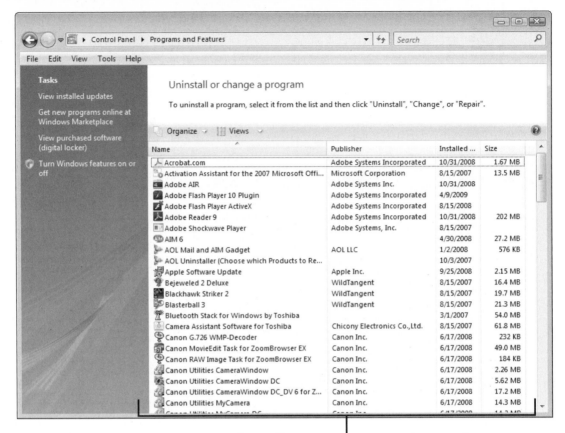

Vista lists all your programs in this window.

Figure 4-9

3. Select the program that you want to uninstall.

4. Click whatever uninstall button the program provides (such as Change, Remove, Change/Remove, or Uninstall/Change; see **Figure 4-10**), and follow any onscreen instructions.

5. Follow any onscreen instructions.

6. Restart your computer if you're prompted to do so.

➡ **Manufacturer utility:** Use a specialized Remove or Uninstall utility that the program's installer put on your computer along with the software program.

Click Remove to delete the selected program in Windows XP.
Figure 4-10

 In some cases, you may have to find an uninstall utility on the CD or DVD that you used to install the program, or you may have to download an uninstall utility from the manufacturer's Web site.

1. Choose Start⇨All Programs (or Programs) to display a list of all the programs on your PC.

2. Select the program you want to uninstall. If you see a right-pointing arrow next to its name, multiple options are available; place the mouse pointer on the arrow to expand the menu, and choose the uninstall option.

3. Follow any onscreen instructions.

4. Restart your computer if you're prompted to do so.

➠ **Manual deletion:** Delete the program from your hard drive manually; then search for and remove all its interconnections with Windows and other programs.

 Brute-force removal of components is not recommended — at least, not for an unassisted amateur. Merely deleting a program from your hard disk doesn't remove all its interconnections with other applications and may do more harm than good.

Practicing Good Computer Hygiene

*T*he best repair is the one you don't have to make. If you can keep your computer up to date and in tune, you and your PC will live happier, more productive lives.

The best defense against aging or sudden death is keeping your computer cool, calm, and collected. By that, I mean ensuring that it doesn't overheat; that it's protected from electrical surges; that the logical parts are efficiently organized; and that the programs aren't scrambled, garbled, or improperly altered.

In this chapter, I talk about preventive and diagnostic measures that help you keep your computer in good health and spot problems before they become serious. Think of this chapter as providing vitamin pills, medical scans, and a safe deposit box for your PC.

Run the System Configuration Utility

1. Follow the appropriate step for your version of Windows:

- **Windows XP:** Choose Start⊳Run to open the Run dialog box, type **msconfig** in the Open text box, and press Enter.

- **Vista and Windows 7:** Click the Start button, type **msconfig** in the Search Programs and Files field at the bottom of the screen, and press Enter; then click Msconfig in the resulting list.

Whichever method you use, the System Configuration dialog box opens (see **Figure 5-1**).

Click a tab to view related settings.

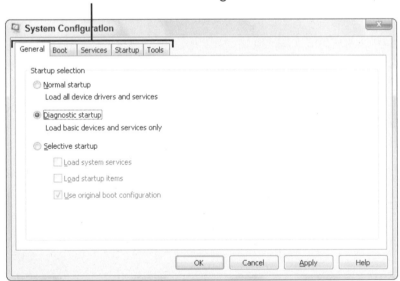

Figure 5-1

2. Select Diagnostic Startup on the General tab and then click OK. The System Configuration utility takes a few moments to disable all but the most necessary applications that run at startup; then it displays a Restart dialog box.

3. Click Restart to restart your computer in diagnostic mode. In Windows XP, you see a message reminding you that diagnostic mode is active. In Vista and Windows 7, note the change in the Start button; the text-only button indicates diagnostic mode.

4. Click OK to close the message and launch System Configuration. In Vista and Windows 7 you have to relaunch this utility as described above.

5. Leave the utility running, and test your system.

Some things, such as custom Internet Explorer toolbars, may not run during testing because the System Configuration utility disables them.

6. Click the Services tab, and scroll through the list of software services that run each time your computer starts, looking for suspect applications: those from unknown manufacturers or those with names that don't seem to fit anything you're using.

Most of the services in this list will show the manufacturer as Microsoft, and most of them will be disabled. You can probably ignore those services.

7. Make only one change at a time.

8. On the General tab of the System Configuration dialog box, select Normal Startup, and click OK. When your computer restarts, see whether you've corrected the problem.

9. If the problem persists, repeat Steps 1–8, adding new applications one at a time. If the problem returns after you add an application, you've found the software that is causing it. Contact the manufacturer, or download an update from the Internet.

10. Click the Startup tab (see **Figure** 5-2), and conduct a similar inspection and test.

Study this list, and reenable applications one at a time.

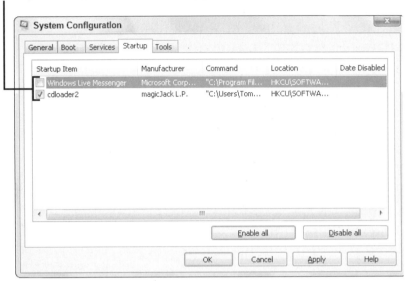

Figure 5-2

11. Review the list of additional utilities available on the Tools tab. To use one of these programs, select it and then click the Launch button at the bottom of the dialog box.

System Configuration is a useful tool that may help you uncover problems and certainly will give you information about your system. Use it cautiously, however. I recommend that you stay away from the .INI tab in Windows XP and the Boot and Services tabs in Vista and Windows; you could change something on these tabs that would make your computer unusable.

Run Microsoft Office Diagnostics

1. Close all running applications, including Microsoft Office applications. You shouldn't try to use your computer while the diagnostics utility is running.

2. Choose Start⇨Programs⇨All Programs⇨Microsoft Office.

3. Select Office Tools and then click Microsoft Office Diagnostics to display the opening dialog box shown in **Figure 5-3**.

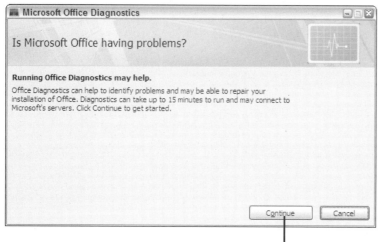

Click Continue to launch a series of health-check utilities.
Figure 5-3

4. Click the Continue button to start the diagnostics routines, which test items including the following:

- Microsoft Office setup and configuration

- Hard drive health and function

- System memory (RAM)

- Program compatibility

- Known solutions

5. Follow any onscreen instructions.

Clean Up Your Hard Drive

1. Choose Start➪All Programs➪Accessories.

2. Select System Tools, and click Disk Cleanup to open the Disk Cleanup dialog box (see **Figure** 5-4).

Choose the files you want to remove.

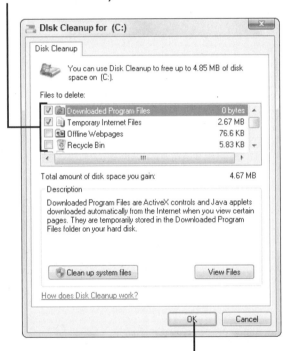

Click OK to start the cleanup process.

Figure 5-4

3. In the Files to Delete list, check the boxes next to the names of the files you want to remove, and clear the boxes next to any files you want to keep.

4. Click the Clean Up System Files button to expand the list of files you can remove safely, such as error reports and log files.

5. Click the More Options tab (which appears after you click Clean Up System Files in Step 4) to clean up programs you don't use or to remove System Restore files.

 You should remove System Restore files (see Chapter 16) and shadow copies only if you're desperate for hard drive space. These files can help you get your system back to normal if the current installation files become damaged or your configuration gets out of whack.

6. Click OK to start the cleanup process.

7. When Windows asks you whether you're sure that you want to delete these files, click Yes.

 You should run Disk Cleanup before you run the Disk Defragmenter utility (see the next section) so the regained disk space will be defragmented too.

Defragment Your Hard Drive

1. Choose Start➪All Programs➪Accessories.

2. Select System Tools, and click Disk Defragmenter to open the Disk Defragmenter dialog box (see **Figure** 5-5).

- **Vista and Windows 7:** This dialog box automatically shows you the percentage of fragmentation on the selected hard drive; proceed to Step 3.

- **Windows XP:** Click the Analyze Disk button to display a complete report on your hard drive, including the percentage of fragmentation; then proceed to Step 3.

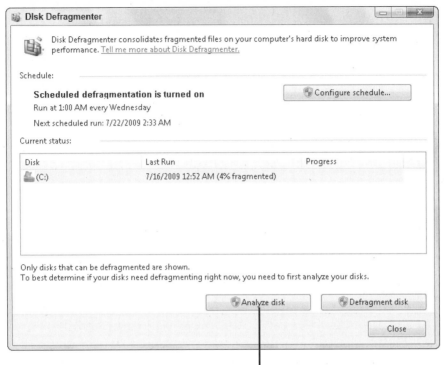

Click Analyze Disk to produce a report on the selected drive.

Figure 5-5

3. Check the fragmentation report to decide whether you need to defragment the selected drive. A drive with 10 percent or more fragmentation should be defragmented. (If you've been using your computer for a while, the drive may show 50 percent fragmentation or more.)

4. To defragment the selected drive, quit any other running programs and then click the Defragment Disk button. This process can be lengthy, and you really shouldn't be running any other software while Defragmenter works, because you could be creating and saving files while the utility is trying to consolidate them.

In Windows XP, you have to remember to run the Defragmenter utility periodically. In Vista and Windows 7, by default, the utility runs automatically on all connected hard drives once a week. To set your own defragmentation schedule, click the Configure Schedule button in the Disk Defragmenter dialog box.

Test for Chinks in the Security Armor

 You can find lots of free security tools online. I recommend ShieldsUP!, which sends a series of probes to see which ports (think of them as doors; see Chapter 2) are open on your computer and what details you're telling the world about yourself or your personal and business secrets. This tool won't fix the problems that it finds, but it will give you some indication of whether the security program you have installed is doing an adequate job or needs adjustment.

1. Point your Web browser to the Gibson Research Web site at **www.grc.com.**

2. Click the ShieldsUP! logo.

3. In the resulting page, scroll down to and click the ShieldsUP! link.

4. Review the opening screen, which shows you the information about your Internet connection that's presented when you visit a Web site.

5. Click the Proceed button to display a list of services (see **Figure 5-6**). To get more information on any service, click the Explain This to Me link.

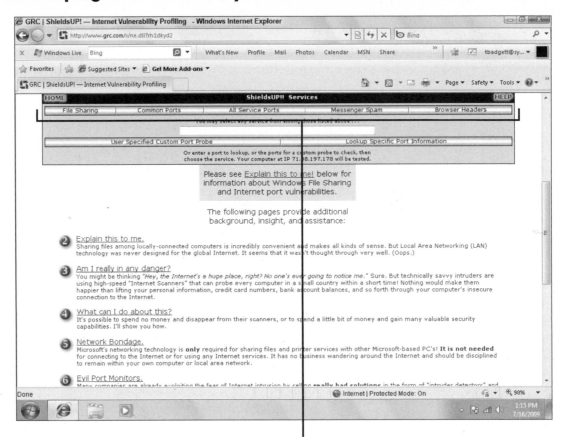

Click a service button to begin a test.

Figure 5-6

6. Click a service name to start a scan of your computer. **Figure 5-7** shows the beginning of a Service Ports probe, which tests the first 1,056 ports. (I've obscured the details about my computer shown at the top of the scan. You understand why, don't you?)

7. Study the finished-test display. All boxes green is a perfect score, meaning that all your PC's ports are secure.

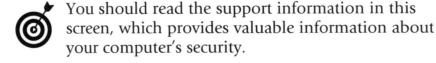 You should read the support information in this screen, which provides valuable information about your computer's security.

Hover your mouse pointer over a port square for more information.

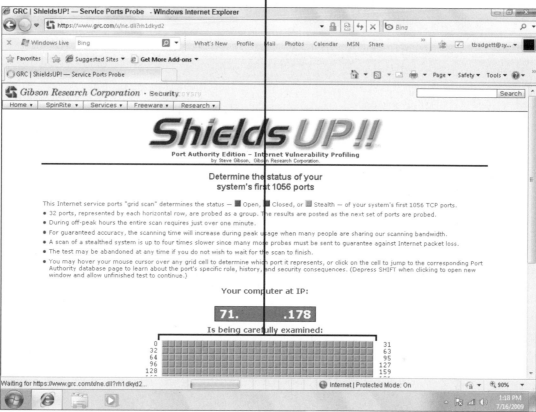

Figure 5-7

Keep Things Cool

➠ **Check the vents.** Make certain that the intake and exhaust vents on your computer aren't blocked. Most vents are on the back of the computer; if you have a PC with that design, don't place the back of it flush against a wall or curtains.

➠ **Clean the vents.** Every few months, use a handheld vacuum to remove dust buildup on the intake and exhaust vents.

➠ **Check airflow.** Once a week (more often if your computer starts to crash or otherwise becomes unreliable), check the flow of air coming out of your computer by placing your hand near the vent. The air should feel warm but not painfully hot. If you don't feel air coming out of the exhaust vent, follow these steps:

1. Visually inspect the fan housing on the back of your computer (see Chapter 2). If the fan isn't turning, the motor may be bad, or a power connector may be unplugged. If the fan is turning, but little or no air is coming out, something may be clogging the air path.

2. Shut down the computer.

3. Unplug the power cord and any other cables that could block your access inside the computer.

4. Place the computer on a sturdy, well-lighted work surface, and open the case (see Chapter 2). See this book's information about grounding yourself.

5. If the fan wasn't turning in Step 1, make sure that its power connector is attached securely. If it isn't, fix the connection. If the connection's already secure, you probably need a new fan. Contact a computer repair facility.

6. Carefully feel for hot spots, and look for blockages in the thermal tunnel that runs (in most modern cases) from the front to the rear of the unit (see **Figure 5-8**).

7. Use a vacuum cleaner or a small, *clean* paintbrush to remove dust inside the case. Pay particular attention to the louvers around the outside of the case where air is supposed to enter the enclosure.

Check both ends of this tunnel for dust, which could restrict airflow.

Figure 5-8

 You should keep the inside and outside of your computer case clean, but the components are delicate. Use caution with a vacuum cleaner or brush! You don't want to disconnect any wires or damage anything.

8. Look for additional fans. Many computers have multiple cooling fans, and they all need to work to provide proper cooling.

9. Close the case, and hook everything back up.

10. Turn on the computer, and recheck airflow.

➡ **Check the fans.** Look and listen to determine whether the power-supply fan and any auxiliary fans are running. If small auxiliary fans have stopped working, you should replace them; if the power-supply fan isn't working, you should replace the entire power-supply unit. See Chapter 9 for details on both procedures.

Mind Your Monitor

➡ **Use a surge protector.** Never plug your display directly into wall current. Instead, be sure to use a good-quality surge protector (see Chapter 1). Damage caused by an electrical spike ordinarily isn't covered by manufacturer warranties.

➡ **Keep the air vents open.** Never cover the air vents on the top or sides of a monitor. Doing so could result in a dangerous buildup of heat that could damage components or shorten their lives. Periodically, use a new paintbrush or the brush attachment of a vacuum cleaner to remove accumulated dust on the monitor's ventilation holes.

➡ **Leave it on.** The most dangerous moment in an electronic component's life is when power is first applied, and the component goes from cold and uncharged to warm and full of electricity. Avoid turning your monitor on and off more than necessary. You can reduce power consumption by following these steps:

1. Right-click your desktop, and choose Properties (Windows XP) or Personalize (Vista and Windows 7) from the shortcut menu.

2. Follow the appropriate step for your version of Windows:

   • **Windows XP:** Click the Screen Saver tab of the Properties dialog box.

   • **Vista and Windows 7:** Click the Screen Saver tab of the Personalize dialog box; then click Change Power Settings.

   Whichever method you use, you see the dialog box shown in **Figure 5-9.**

Click to set the time delay.

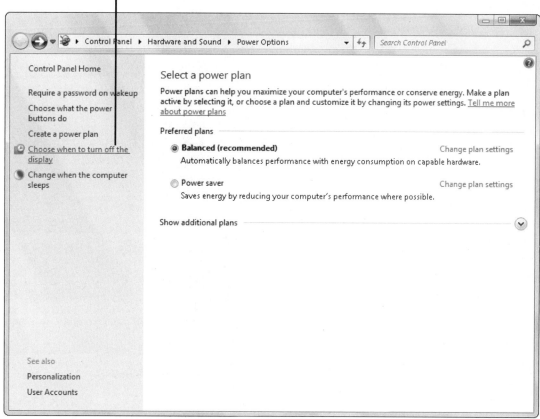

Figure 5-9

3. Click Choose When to Turn Off the Display to set the
time delay before Windows turns off your monitor.
You also can set system sleep delay and some other
options in this dialog box.

Vista and Windows 7 have preprogrammed power-
saving settings. You can accept one of these settings
or customize the times.

➠ **Check the connections.** Make sure that the cable
between the monitor and the video card is firmly
attached at each end and not crimped or pinched. If
you need to make adjustments, follow these steps:

1. If your monitor has a removable cable, unplug it and then replug it into the receptacle on the monitor (see **Figure 5-10**). This step could reset a loose connection and remove corrosion on any of the connectors.

Unplug and reset all cables.

Figure 5-10

2. Unplug and reconnect the monitor cable at the computer end. You may have to use a screwdriver or thumbscrew to unlock the connection before you can unplug it. Use these locking screws when you replug the cable.

➠ **Klutzproof it.** Be sure that the monitor is safely installed on a sturdy desk, with its cable properly out of tripping range of passersby. I don't have to warn you about placing cups of coffee or soda anywhere in the vicinity, right?

Pamper Your Printer

➠ **Keep it squeaky-clean.** Read the instructions that come with your printer, and follow the recommended cleaning cycles.

- **Inkjet printers:** For an inkjet, cleaning usually involves keeping the nozzles clear through regular use or by running a built-in cleaning program.

 If you don't expect to use an inkjet printer for several months, you may want to remove the ink cartridge (or each ink cartridge, in the case of color printers) and store it in a closed case so that it won't dry out. **Figure 5-11** shows a typical inkjet printer with instructions for changing cartridges under the lid.

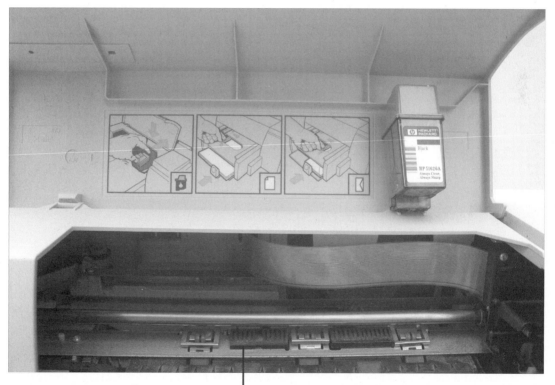

Open your printer case, and follow the directions for replacing cartidges.
Figure 5-11

- **Laser printers:** Follow the manufacturer's cleaning instructions, which may include careful vacuuming of the interior of the machine, and keep the internal drum away from direct sunlight and extreme temperatures.

→ **Control the humidity.** Many printers are prone to paper jams and quality problems in times of high humidity.

 One solution for the summertime blues: Keep your paper in a sealed plastic box, and load it into the printer tray only when it's needed.

Keeping Intruders out of Your Computer

How can a box of metal, silicon, and plastic parts be laid low? Consider the following ills that computers are heir to:

➠ **Viruses:** A computer *virus* or other condition that falls under the broad term *malware* is an infection that takes over Windows or another program, making your computer do something you don't want it to do.

➠ **Spyware:** *Spyware,* which is another form of malware, hides on your computer and watches everything on it: the Web sites you visit, your login names and passwords for banking, even the text you compose for e-mails and instant messages.

➠ **Phishing** (pronounced *fishing)*: This electronic con game tricks computer users into revealing valuable information such as bank account or credit card numbers. The most common form is an e-mail that appears to come from your bank or credit card company, asking you to update your account or provide additional information.

➠ **Spam:** *Spam* is electronic junk mail, unwanted advertisements, or just plain @!*^%&# that arrives in your inbox. Besides being annoying, it can expose you to the risk of downloading malware.

In this chapter, I give you pointers on defending your PC from all these security breaches.

Play Smart Defense

➠ **Be legal.** Buy and use only legal copies of all software on your computer, and register your name and e-mail address with the makers. To put it another way, don't buy or use bootleg copies of software, and be very cautious about using software offered by companies or people you don't know and trust.

➠ **Stay current.** Keep all software up to date, installing updates and patches as the manufacturer releases them. (For details on updating software, see Chapter 4.)

➠ **Install security.** Install a capable antivirus or comprehensive security package, and use it regularly to scan your computer (see "Check for Viruses," later in this chapter).

Your Internet service provider may offer antivirus or security protection as part of your service package. Comcast, for example, offers the McAfee antivirus program (see **Figure 6-1**).

➠ **Take advice.** Follow the manufacturers' recommended security settings for Windows, your Internet browser, and your security software.

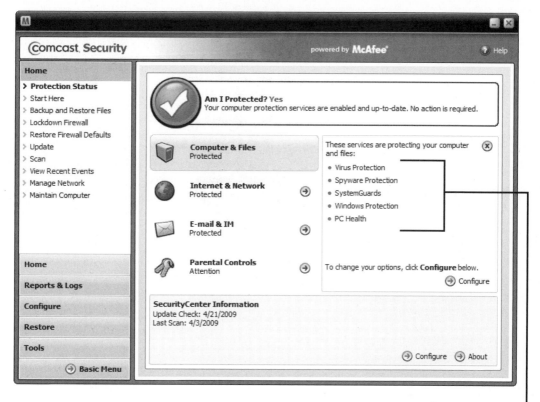

Security services

Figure 6-1

Configure Windows Security Center

1. Choose Start➪Control Panel to open the Control Panel window.

2. Follow the appropriate step for your version of Windows:

- **Windows XP and Vista:** In Classic View, double-click the Security Center icon.

- **Windows 7:** In Classic (icon) View, click Action Center and then choose Security. In Category View, click System and Security; then click Action Center and choose Security.

Whichever method you use, Windows Security Center opens, displaying an opening screen similar to the one shown in **Figure** 6-2.

Click to get more information online.

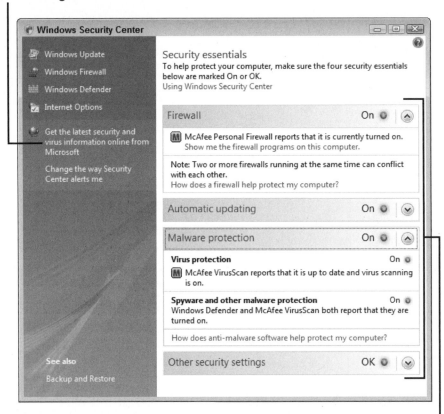

Note the settings for Security Center's monitored areas.

Figure 6-2

3. Study this screen to understand what Windows Security Center is monitoring and make sure that your computer is protected. If all sections are marked On or green, Security Center is configured properly, and crucial security software is running.

Vista and Windows 7 also include an Other Security Settings section, where you can check the status of User Account Control (UAC) and Network Access Protection (NAP). UAC lets you know when programs try to make changes in your computer. NAP, which is for corporate networks, verifies individual computer configurations and manages automatic updates.

Build a Firewall in Windows

1. Choose Start⇨Control Panel to open the Control Panel window.

2. Follow the appropriate step for your version of Windows:

- **Windows XP:** In Classic View, double-click the Windows Firewall icon.

- **Vista and Windows 7:** In Classic View, click Windows Firewall. In Category View, click System and Security and then select Windows Firewall.

Whichever method you use, Windows Firewall opens, displaying a screen like the one shown in **Figure 6-3**.

 A *public network* is simply one that anyone can access without entering a passcode. This type of network may be in your home or at a business. Unless you live in a remote area, your home network should be passcode-protected. This topic is beyond the scope of this book; for full details, see *Home Networking For Dummies*, 4th Edition, by Kathy Ivens (Wiley Publishing).

Click these links to configure your firewall.

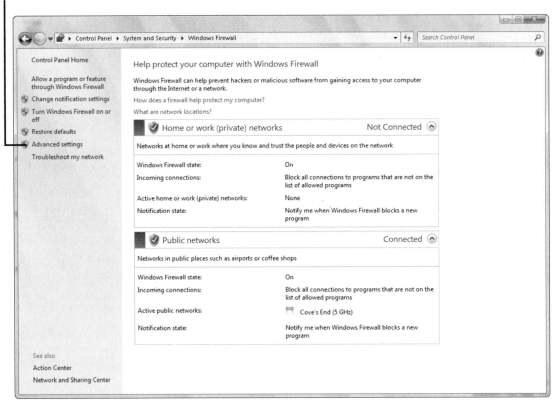

Figure 6-3

3. If you need to expand access through the firewall, click the Allow a Program or Feature through Windows Firewall link. Certain applications, such as Windows Live Sync, are given expanded access automatically, but you may also want to give access to devices such as cell-phones or media players, or to a custom business or personal application.

4. Click Turn Windows Firewall On or Off if you want to disable the firewall completely for testing or to allow specific one-time access. (Just remember to turn the firewall back on when you finish.)

If you prefer, you can use a separate firewall product or one that's built into a third-party security program. Follow the manufacturer's instructions about using the firewall product on a PC that also has Windows Firewall installed.

Check for Viruses

If your computer doesn't have a capable, up-to-date antivirus or broader Internet security program, *stop reading right now.* Go get one of these programs, install it, and give your computer a full scan. Be sure to follow the instructions carefully. Some manufacturers set up their antivirus products so that they scan your system before they're installed; others take over after they're in place.

1. Make sure that you always have the latest updates for your antivirus or security program. Some programs check for and download updates automatically based on a schedule that you set. You can always check for updates manually as long as you do so regularly (see **Figure** 6-4).

2. Every week or so, use the program to scan your computer for viruses.

Run the program any time things suddenly go strange on your computer — if files are missing or renamed, for example, or if your Internet home page has changed without your knowledge. Do this even if you scanned your PC recently, because viruses can attack at any time.

3. If your computer's antivirus or Internet security program displays an ominous warning, follow the onscreen instructions carefully to remove or quarantine the threat. Many security-software makers offer specific tools for removing particular virus strains that broke out into the wild despite precautions by computer users.

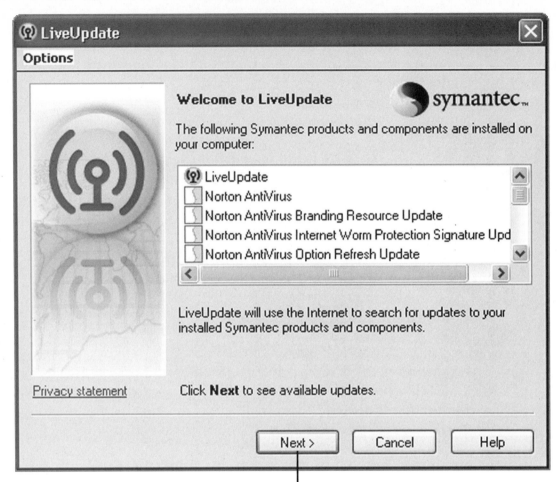

Click to check for security and antivirus updates.

Figure 6-4

Fight Malware

➠ **Inspect e-mail before opening it.** Pay attention to the details of an e-mail before you open it. Be especially cautious about e-mails that are addressed to `undisclosed-recipients` or to a name you don't recognize, and about e-mails that have a blank or odd Subject line. Anything you receive by e-mail that seems too good to be true probably is (see **Figure 6-5**).

E-mail that's not addressed to you personally means
spam at least and possibly something more nefarious

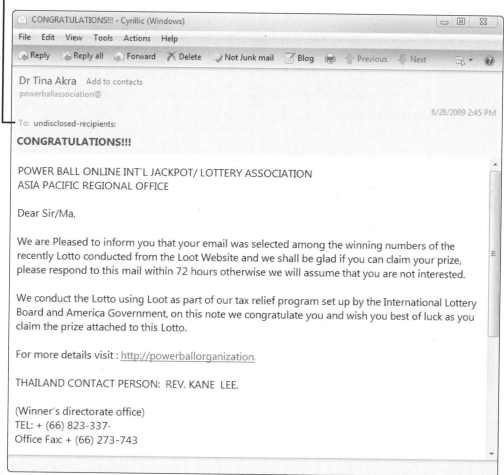

Figure 6-5

 If you receive an e-mail from someone you don't
know, the best thing to do is delete it without opening it. Also, never follow a link in an e-mail unless
you're sure where it goes.

➡ **Be wary of attachments.** Never open an attachment
to an e-mail or to an instant message (IM) unless
you know and trust the source — and even then, ask
yourself whether the risk is worth the reward.

If you do decide to accept an attachment of any kind — music, video, a picture, or any other type of file — use an antivirus or security program to scan it before opening it (see "Check for Viruses," earlier in this chapter).

➡ **Be leery of links.** If you receive an e-mail or IM with an embedded Web link, don't click that link within the message. If you decide that visiting the Web site in question is worth your time (and the risk), copy the link to your computer's clipboard and then paste it into your Web browser's address bar. This method gives your Internet security program a better chance to block a malicious Web site or identify other problems with the link.

➡ **Message with care.** When you're connected to an IM session, be on the lookout for strange or inappropriate messages, links, or offers of downloads. A person with bad intentions may have managed to obtain the password and login information of someone you know or otherwise found a way to pose as someone else. End the IM session immediately if something strange happens, and consider notifying the provider of the IM service.

➡ **Avoid autorun.** Turn off the autorun feature that automatically starts the execution of programs on memory sticks and other USB devices (see Chapter 2). In Vista and Windows 7, you have a lot of control in this area. Just follow these steps:

1. Choose Start➪Control Panel to open the Control Panel window.

2. Click Hardware and Sound and then click AutoPlay to display a screen like the one shown in **Figure 6-6.**

For maximum security, choose Ask Me Every Time for all media.

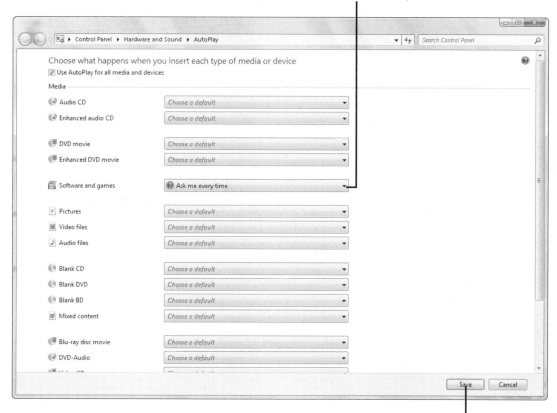

Click Save after making changes.

Figure 6-6

3. Make a new choice from the drop-down menu for any medium you want to change. (Notice that by default, Software and Games is set to Ask Me Every Time. It's probably safe to autoplay DVDs and audio CDs, but if you have any doubts, leave this menu set to the default.)

4. Click the Save button to save your changes.

In Windows XP, you don't have this level of control, but you can make some changes in the Internet Options dialog box, which you access by choosing Start⇨Control Panel⇨Internet Options. Click the Security tab, scroll down to select Prompt under Launching Applications and Unsafe Files, and then click OK.

Stop Spyware

➠ **Block secret transmissions.** Set your firewall (see "Build a Firewall in Windows," earlier in this chapter) to block any requests by a program to send outgoing messages without your permission.

➠ **Click Internet ads rarely and carefully.** Be very selective about clicking online advertisements. When you open an ad, you're communicating with a Web site, and that communication may trigger the download of malware.

➠ **Turn off e-mail previews and automatic downloads.** Most capable e-mail programs allow you to turn off automatic previews and downloads of e-mail contents. **Figure 6-7** shows the option that you'd disable in Microsoft Outlook Express.

➠ **Beware of unusual error messages on the Internet.** A Web site may warn you that your computer is at risk or request your permission to download a free utility. Unless you asked for this sort of assistance — and also know and trust the source — close both the Web page and your Web browser without accepting the offer.

➠ **Don't take software from strangers.** Be very careful about accepting any offer of free software. The program you receive may not be what you want, or it may deliver hidden malware along with a useful function.

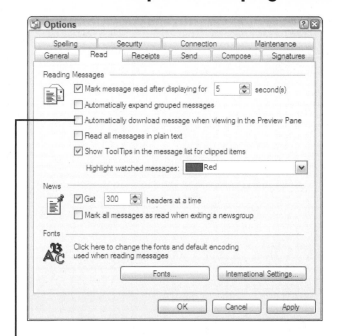

Clear this check box to turn off automatic downloading.

Figure 6-7

 When you install a new piece of software, take the time to read all the installation options carefully. Some options may install features that you don't want — and that may be contaminated with other things you don't want.

➠ **Heed all security warnings.** Pay attention to any warnings that you receive from your Internet security program (see "Check for Viruses," earlier in this chapter). It may notify you that a Web site is attempting to install spyware on your computer or that a program already on your PC is trying to send information to someone else. Accept the security program's recommended action to block or delete the security threat.

Avoid Getting Hooked by Phishers

➠ **Use an Internet security program that trawls for phishers.** Programs such as Norton Internet Security add a notification bar to your Web browser to tell you whether you've reached a properly registered Web site or a phony/hijacked site, and display reports such as the one shown in **Figure 6-8**. These programs also scan incoming e-mails and block known attempts at phishing or notify you of dangerous communications.

Antiphishing report

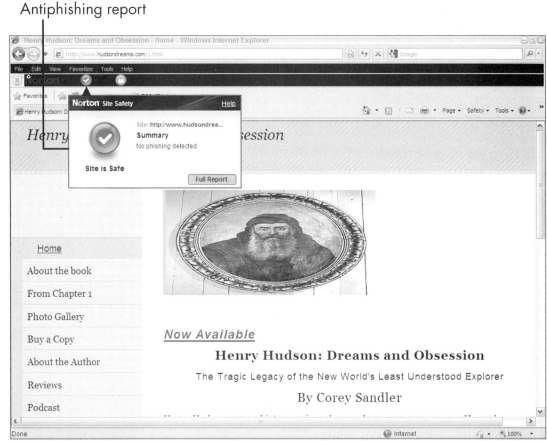

Figure 6-8

➠ **Look up phone numbers yourself.** If you receive a suspicious e-mail that appears to be from your bank or other financial institution, don't call any phone number listed in the message. Instead, call the purported sender by using a number that you obtain from your own bills, invoices, or cards.

➠ **Don't believe everything you see.** A site or message may use official-looking logos and legal-sounding language to reassure you of its legitimacy. Don't be fooled. Logos and legalese can be copied from real communications or simply fabricated. Also don't be fooled by statements in an e-mail or on a Web site that the communication has been scanned by antivirus or security software. Those statements can be faked too.

➠ **Beware of any unsolicited request for your login info.** A common phishing tactic is an e-mail that tells you to click a link to update your financial information; otherwise, your accounts will be canceled. A legitimate Web site may require you to change your information from time to time — but always on the Web site itself and only after you've already logged in.

➠ **Read the fine print on Web sites.** Visit the Web sites of companies that you regularly do business with, and look for security warnings and other information posted there. Most legitimate companies are very quick to post warnings and specific advice about phishing attempts and other scams aimed at their customers.

If you realize (or suspect) that you've been duped by a phisher, treat the situation as though your wallet had just been stolen. Immediately notify all your credit card issuers and financial institutions, placing calls to numbers that you have on file from their official documents.

Can That Spam

➠ **Maintain e-mail security.** Install an Internet security program that includes filtering and blocking utilities for e-mail, and keep it current (see "Check for Viruses," earlier in this chapter).

➠ **When in doubt, throw it out.** Don't open a suspect message. Just delete it. If you open one by accident, however, never click any links in it, and never, ever respond to it.

➠ **Know who your online friends are.** If you use an IM service, reject any messages from people you don't know. Most services allow you to create buddy lists for that purpose (see **Figure 6-9**). Unfortunately, marketers, promoters, salespeople, and crooks can find your ID and make themselves your buddy in an effort to reach you. Delete any name in your buddy list that you don't recognize.

Check your buddy list whenever you open your IM program.

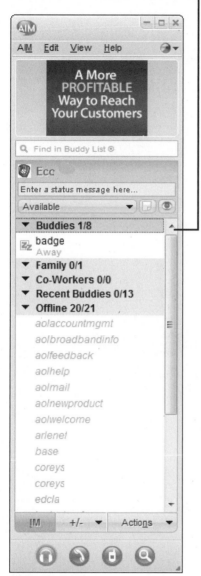

Figure 6-9

Getting Help When Prevention Fails

What a terrible question to have to answer: Should a valued, trusted computer live or die? The economics of personal computing, however, mean that a heroic effort to keep a wounded or dying machine alive isn't always the rational answer.

As you ponder this existential issue, consider these facts:

➧ Every few months, a new wave of computers arrives, and the new models are faster, better, and often less expensive than the ones that came before.

➧ In terms of monetary value, the whole of a PC is considerably less than the sum of its parts.

➧ Forget about the hardware, and think about any data stored on your computer that's not also safely stored on a backup disk or drive. To borrow an aphorism from a credit card commercial: A brand-new PC, $500. Your letters, e-mails, and photos, priceless.

In this chapter, I point you to sources of help for an ailing computer and give you some tips to help with the repair-or-replace decision.

Identify the Problem: Hardware or Software

 For information on diagnosing and repairing hardware, see the appropriate chapters in Part III. Software remedies are often specific to the program, but I provide some general tips in Chapter 4. Also see Part IV for fixes for your PC's operating system (Windows).

➡ **Hardware failure:** When hardware fails, it usually can be replaced. Notice that I don't say *repaired*. Modern computers have very little hardware that an amateur technician can fix, and the few parts that an expert might be able to repair (such as the motor for a hard disk drive) don't make economic sense to repair . . . unless the value of the data stored on that drive convinces you otherwise. (For more information, see "Weigh the Cost of Repair versus Replacement," later in this chapter.)

Q: How many computer hardware technicians does it take to change a light bulb? **A:** None. That's a software problem. (The light bulb is a replaceable consumable, aka software; the wiring and power grid that support it are permanent hardware.)

If you don't want to go under the hood to replace a hard drive (see Chapter 11), one alternative is attaching a new external hard drive to your PC via its USB port. (**Figure 7-1** shows a typical external hard drive.) You may have to install a device driver provided by the drive's manufacturer, or Windows may recognize the drive and help you configure it.

USB connector   Power connector

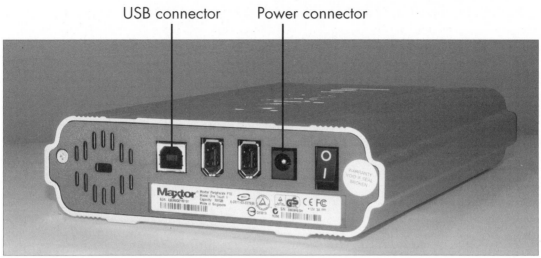

Figure 7-1

➡️ **Software failure:** On the software side, things are different. Almost anything can be fixed, and the process doesn't involve the use of a screwdriver (see Chapter 4). Instead, you can use the advanced features of Windows to fix certain problems or reinstall the operating system or programs when repairs aren't possible.

Find a Helper

➡️ **Computer manufacturers:** In recent years, manufacturers have cut back sharply on their technical support departments or tried to turn what used to be free support service into a source of profit. Still, this option may be worth a try, especially if the computer is still under warranty or if you purchased an extended warranty that's still in effect.

 The time to test manufacturer support is when you're shopping for a new computer. You can start with a support Web page. To get a feel for the type and quality of customer care you'll receive, contact the manufacturer *before* you buy the PC, and ask a question about something you don't understand. If the company doesn't treat you well before it has your money, what makes you think that it'll be helpful after your check has cleared?

 Sometimes it's worthwhile to pay a bit extra to obtain an extended warranty or access to technical support. Make sure that you understand the terms, however. Ask whether the company will assist you with any problem, even if it's related to hardware or software that you add on your own or to the operating system.

➡ **Computer repair services:** I'm more than a little wary of dealing with many third-party computer repair services. Investigate them — and seek recommendations from friends — just as you would before getting an auto repair. Remember that most of these shops charge by the hour and also hope to sell you replacement parts. That combination (and the potential conflict of interest) could cost you a lot of money if the shop isn't good at what it does or honest about the way it conducts business.

➡ **Tech-savvy friends or relatives:** This option may be your best bet. Ask around. Do you have a friend or relative who's capable of repairing a computer? If so, offer him a reasonable *flat fee* to fix your machine — say, $50, a free dinner, or a mention in your will. If your friendly technician recommends replacing a part, pay him the actual cost of getting the part replaced at a reputable store. (Call a few stores to find out what that cost would be.)

 Don't have a nearby friend, relative, or repair shop to fix your computer? No problem — you may be able to get help through Windows Remote Assistance, which I cover in the following sections. Windows

Remote Assistance allows anyone whom you invite — such as a professional technician or a friend who's offered to help — to take control of your computer. The connection between the computers is encrypted to protect your data from interception by snoops on the Internet. In Microsoft lingo, the user asking for help is the *novice*, and the person coming to the rescue is the *expert*.

Get Remote Assistance in Windows XP

 This process is complex enough and different enough in each version of Windows that I can give you only the highlights in this chapter. For full information on using Remote Assistance, go to www.microsoft. com or www.bing.com, search for Windows Remote Assistance, and click the link for your version.

1. Choose Start⇨Help and Support to open the Windows Help and Support window.

2. In the Ask for Assistance section, click Invite a Friend to Connect to Your Computer with Remote Assistance. Windows Remote Assistance opens.

3. Click Invite Someone to Help You.

4. In the next screen, choose the option you want to use to contact your helper: Windows Messenger or e-mail.

5. Follow the step that corresponds with the option you chose in Step 4:

- **Windows Messenger:** Sign into Messenger, enter a contact name and password, and send your helper an IM invitation.

- **E-mail:** In the Use E-Mail section of the resulting dialog box, enter your helper's e-mail address;

then click Invite This Person and follow the
onscreen instructions to fill out and send the
e-mail invitation.

6. When your helper accepts the invitation, a dialog box
pops up on your screen, asking for permission to give
this person access to your computer. Click Yes to start the
Remote Assistance session.

7. The expert will ask to take control of your computer by
clicking a button in her console, and a message will
appear on your screen to tell you about the request. Click
Yes (or, if you change your mind, No).

 When an expert has taken control of the computer,
both ends of the communication share control of the
keyboard and the mouse. To prevent confusion, keep
your hands by your side.

8. Watch carefully to see what the expert is doing. If you
think that she's straying into areas that aren't related to
your problem, end the session in any of the following
ways:

- Click Stop Control.

- Press the Esc key on your keyboard.

- Click Disconnect.

 If you cancel a Remote Assistance session, you can
always reconnect later.

Get Remote Assistance in Vista

1. Choose Start➪Windows Help and Support to open the
Help and Support Window (see **Figure 7-2**).

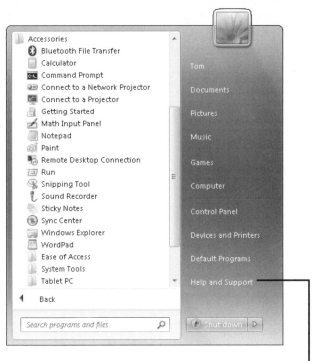

Click this link to start the process.

Figure 7-2

2. In the Invite Someone section, click the Windows Remote Assistance link. Windows Remote Assistance opens (see **Figure 7-3**).

 Another way to display the Remote Assistance window is to choose Start⇨All Programs⇨Maintenance and then select Remote Assistance.

3. Click Invite Someone You Trust to Help You.

4. In the next screen, choose the option you want to use to contact your helper: Windows Messenger or e-mail.

5. Follow the step that corresponds with the option you chose in Step 4:

- **Windows Messenger:** Sign into Messenger, enter a contact name and password, and send your helper an IM invitation.

Invite your helper from this page.

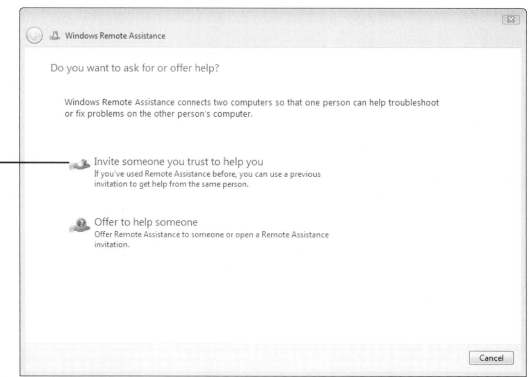

Figure 7-3

- **E-mail:** In the Use E-Mail section of the resulting dialog box, enter your helper's e-mail address; then click Invite This Person and follow the onscreen instructions. Your helper gets an automatic e-mail invitation that's really a file containing all the information (except the password) that your helper needs to find your computer and log in.

6. After you send the invitation, you see the Waiting for Incoming Connection window (see **Figure** 7-4). Leave it open until the person you invited accepts.

Leave this window open until the helper logs on to your computer.

Figure 7-4

7. When your helper accepts the invitation, a dialog box pops up on your screen, asking for permission to give this person access to your computer. Click Yes to start the Remote Assistance session.

8. The expert will ask to take control of your computer by clicking a button in his console, and a message appears on your screen to tell you about the request. Click Yes (or, if you change your mind, No).

 When an expert has taken control of the computer, both ends of the communication share control of the keyboard and the mouse. To prevent confusion, keep your hands by your side.

9. Watch carefully to see what the expert does. If you think that he's straying into areas that aren't related to your problem, end the session in any of the following ways:

- Click Stop Sharing.

- Click Cancel.

- Press Alt+T on your keyboard.

- Choose Settings⇨Use ESC to Stop Sharing Control and then press the Esc key on your keyboard.

 If you cancel a Remote Assistance session, you can always reconnect later.

Get Remote Assistance in Windows 7

1. Choose Start⇨All Programs⇨Maintenance and then select Windows Remote Assistance. Windows Remote Assistance opens.

2. Click Invite Someone You Trust to Help You (see **Figure 7-5**).

Click to invite a helper.

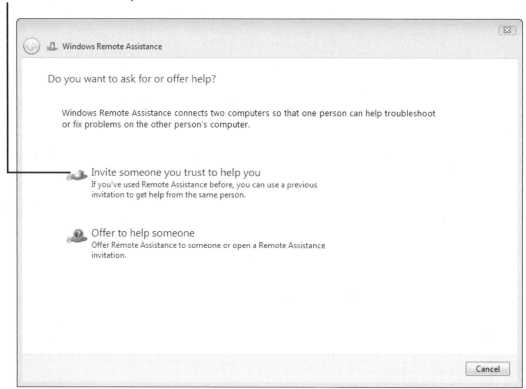

Figure 7-5

 Here's another way to invite a helper: Choose Start⇨ Control Panel, choose System and Security in Category View, click Troubleshoot Computer Problems in Action Center, and then click Get Help from Someone You Trust on the left side of the screen.

3. Choose the way you want to contact your helper: save the invitation as a file, send the invitation as an e-mail, or use Easy Connect.

If you choose to use Easy Connect, which is a Windows 7 utility, your helper must also have access to Easy Connect.

4. Follow the onscreen instructions for whichever method you chose in Step 3 to send the invitation (see **Figure 7-6**).

Sending the invitation as an e-mail

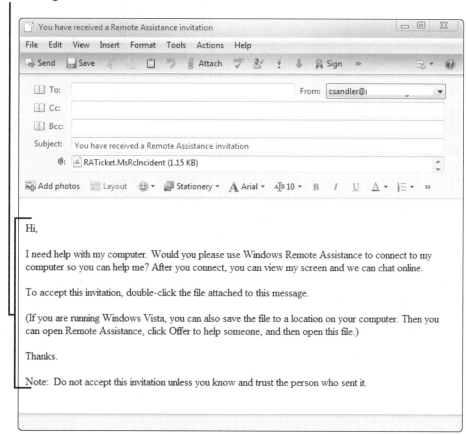

Figure 7-6

5. After you send the invitation, you see the Waiting for Incoming Connection window. Leave it open until the person you invited accepts.

6. When your helper accepts the invitation, a dialog box pops up on your screen, asking for permission to give this person access to your computer. Click Yes to start the Remote Assistance session.

7. The expert will ask to take control of your computer by clicking a button in her console, and a message appears on your screen to tell you about the request. Click Yes (or, if you change your mind, No).

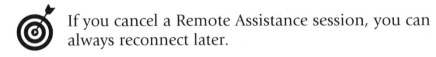 When an expert has taken control of the computer, both ends of the communication share control of the keyboard and the mouse. To prevent confusion, keep your hands by your side.

8. Watch carefully to see what the expert is doing. If you think that she's straying into areas that aren't related to your problem, end the session in any of the following ways:

- Click Stop Sharing.

- Press Alt+T on your keyboard.

- Choose Settings⇨Use ESC to Stop Sharing Control and then press the Esc key on your keyboard.

If you cancel a Remote Assistance session, you can always reconnect later.

Weigh the Cost of Repair versus Replacement

1. Calculate the difference between what you'd spend for a new computer and what you'd spend for the replacement parts you need:

- **Fully equipped new computer:** In this chapter's introduction, I mention that the cost of a modern PC is almost always much less than the sum of its parts. A fully equipped computer may cost $500 and would include a fresh version of Windows.

- **Parts sold separately:** Compared with purchasing a new PC, buying all the parts separately would cost . . . well, you can do the math yourself.

  Replacement motherboard with microprocessor: $200–$400

  Memory module, 2GB of RAM: $25–$50

  Hard disk drive, 500GB: $50–$75

  CD/DVD drive: $40

  Power supply: $30–$50

  Computer case (see **Figure 7-7**): $50

  Keyboard and mouse: $20–$50

  Windows operating system: $100–$200

  Basic applications: may vary from $40–$150 to replace or upgrade

 Here's the value of looking at a computer in this way: If you have a reasonably current PC, and a couple of fairly inexpensive parts fail (such as the power supply, keyboard, and/or hard drive), it probably makes sense to repair what's broken.

2. Apply the *50 percent rule*, which states that if the cost of repairs (including any labor costs you may choose to pay to an expert) is less than half the price of a new machine, a fix-up job may make sense. On the other hand, if the motherboard fails, you're probably looking at a repair that crosses the 50 percent yardline. (By the way, if a motherboard gets fried, the power supply and memory modules often are damaged as well and need to be replaced.)

You can start with a bare-bones case and add the essentials–at a cost.

Figure 7-7

The 50 percent rule should also apply to extended warranties and support. I wouldn't consider it rational to pay more than half the cost of a new PC for technical support.

3. Consider one very important exception to the 50 percent rule: If your hard disk drive fails, and you don't have backups of your irreplaceable data, it may make sense to pay hundreds of dollars to a professional disk-rescue company, which often (but not always) can extract data from failed drives.

 To find a hard-disk rescue company, search the Internet for *hard disk data recovery.* Typical fees are $200–$400.

Part III

Fixing Sick Hardware

The 5th Wave   By Rich Tennant

"It's amazing how they always fell asleep
during 'Matlock,' but this is their third hour
surfing forensic Web sites."

Repairing the Monitor

*W*ith the birth of the personal computer, we've all come to use the monitor (or display) as the window into the hard electronic soul of the device. A monitor lets us read words, look at images, and (together with a graphical user interface such as the Windows operating system) move things around or issue commands.

In Chapter 1, I explain the distinction between the two main kinds of computer monitors:

➠ **CRT** (cathode ray tube), which is like an old-style television set

➠ **LCD** (liquid crystal display), which is used in most flat-panel TVs and laptop computers

Though LCDs have just about completely replaced CRTs, there's no good reason to change the terms you use for them. You can call these devices either *monitors* or *displays,* as I do in this book; people will get the picture either way.

I don't need to get very technical here. After a monitor is connected to your computer, there's very little to do with it other than sit back and watch it work.

Chapter

8

Get ready to . . .

But what do you do when the lights won't go on? In this chapter, I show you how to fix some common problems with monitors.

Check the Display

1. If your display won't display, make sure that it's turned on. Nearly all units have an indicator light to show that they're receiving power. Sometimes the light glows one color when the power is on but no signal is being received (amber or red, usually) and another color when it is getting a signal (probably green or blue).

2. If the monitor is turned on but the indicator light isn't lit, examine the power cord to make sure that it's connected to both the monitor and its source of power. (If you have an LCD screen, you may have to check three or four plugs connecting the wall outlet, the power adapter, and the display.)

3. Make certain that power is flowing through the wall outlet. The best test is to plug in a radio or lamp that you know is working. If the outlet isn't supplying power, it may be connected to a turned-off wall switch (a connection you should avoid for computers and monitors), or the circuit may be dead because of a blown circuit breaker or other electrical problem.

4. If you have an older CRT, check the brightness, contrast, and other manual controls. Someone — any children or mischievous coworkers in the vicinity? — may have turned those dials or buttons all the way off. (Newer CRTs and all modern LCDs make their adjustments through onscreen utilities accessible from the keyboard.)

5. If everything so far is fine, check for the following problems:

- **Monitor failure (CRT):** A CRT monitor uses high voltage and somewhat delicate transformers and other parts. Its electronics eventually wear out — or can be fried by electrical surges or undervoltage (brownouts).

 Turn your monitor off and wait about 30 seconds; then turn the monitor back on. Watch and listen carefully. Did you see any hint of light as the power came on? Did you hear the high voltage energizing the CRT tube? Also, place the back of your hand close to the screen to feel for static electricity. If the monitor passes one or more of these tests, the power supply is working, the monitor has high voltage, and your problem *probably* is in the cable or the computer.

- **Monitor failure (LCD):** An LCD display requires lower voltage than a CRT does and usually has a longer life. The components that are most likely to fail are the backlight (a tiny fluorescent lamp that produces light that shines through the screen) and the thin LCD panel itself, which can get scratched, cut, cracked, or warped.

 With the monitor turned on, press one of the monitor configuration buttons, probably on the front, on the side, or covered by a trap door. (You may need to find your monitor manual to find out which button to push for various adjustments.) You should see a pop-up menu. If you do, the monitor has power, and the screen is working. The problem must be in the cable connection or in your computer.

- **Trouble with video output from your computer:** I cover this situation in "Troubleshoot a Video Adapter" and "Reset a Video Driver," later in this chapter.

- **Trouble with the video connections:** You may find a crimp, break, or other fault in the connectors on the PC or the display, or in the cable that runs between them (see **Figure 8-1**). Video cables should be carefully screwed into place when connector posts are available, and you should make sure that the cables aren't bent, left on top of heat registers, or otherwise endangered.

Check for bent or broken pins at both ends or the coble.

Figure 8-1

 One possible indicator of a problem with a cable or connector on an analog link is the loss of one or two of the primary colors (red, green, and blue) that are combined to produce other hues.

Troubleshoot the Display

1. One way to determine the likely source of problems with a display is to watch carefully as your computer starts up. If the opening screen (see **Figure 8-2** for Vista's) suddenly goes blank or is replaced by an error message, the monitor and its connecting cable are likely working properly. The problem may be either the video adapter on the motherboard or a setting that you changed in the video adapter's driver or in Windows.

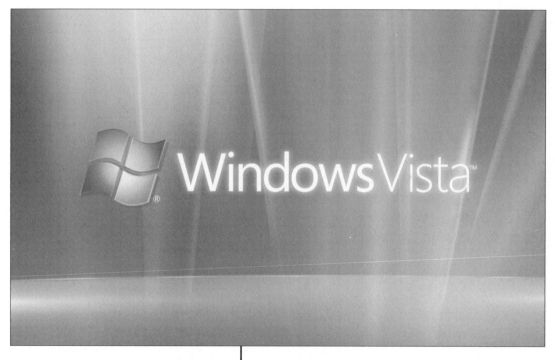

If you see a startup screen in your version of Windows, your monitor and cable probably work.

Figure 8-2

 If you see a blue screen on startup — a condition called the Blue Screen of Death (or Doom) — you have a different problem. See "Beat the Blue Screen of Death," later in this chapter.

2. Restart your computer in safe mode, which automatically uses a very basic video setting. When Windows is loaded, choose Start⇨Control Panel, and change the video settings back to an acceptable set of parameters (see "Check and Change Display Settings," later in this chapter). I explain how to use safe mode in Chapter 17.

3. If Step 2 doesn't help, try attaching the suspect monitor to a computer that you know to be working. (Maybe you have another computer in your home or can take your monitor to a friend's house.) If the monitor delivers the proper image, you know to concentrate your attention on your computer.

4. If your monitor uses a cable that detaches at both ends, swap it with a substitute for a second test. (Some cables, though, are attached permanently at the monitor end.)

 Never attach a cable to a computer that's powered up. A slight misalignment of the plug can produce a short that could damage the video adapter, monitor, motherboard, or all three devices. Turn off both the monitor and the computer before making any cabling changes.

Beat the Blue Screen of Death

1. Start the computer again. If the problem doesn't recur, consider yourself lucky — for the moment. Make backup copies of all your important data files and then check out the computer by using Device Manager and any diagnostics programs provided by the manufacturer. For details on Device Manager, see Chapter 18.

2. Use the Last Known Good Configuration option (see **Figure 8-3**) to restart the PC with settings that were successful recently. See Chapter 16 for details.

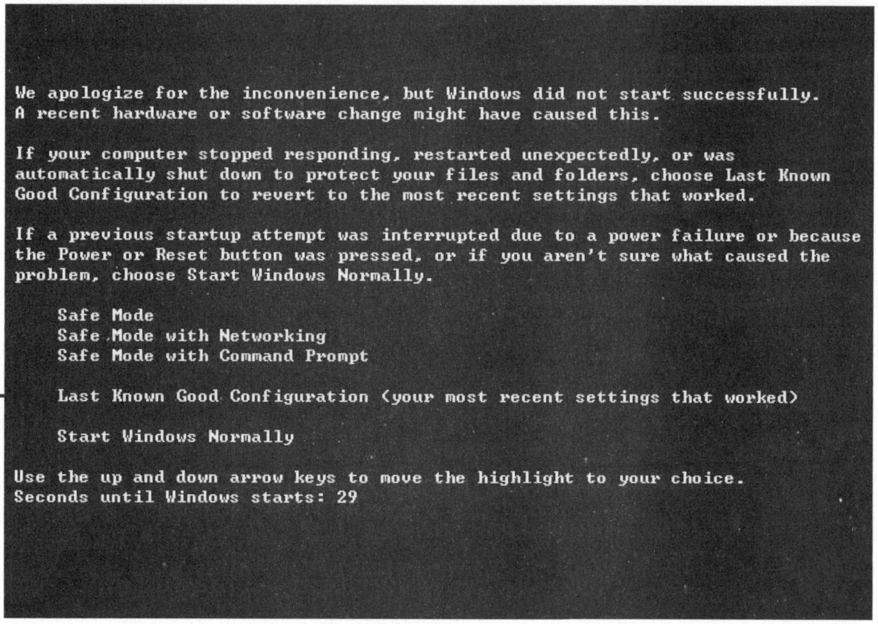

We apologize for the inconvenience, but Windows did not start successfully.
A recent hardware or software change might have caused this.

If your computer stopped responding, restarted unexpectedly, or was
automatically shut down to protect your files and folders, choose Last Known
Good Configuration to revert to the most recent settings that worked.

If a previous startup attempt was interrupted due to a power failure or because
the Power or Reset button was pressed, or if you aren't sure what caused the
problem, choose Start Windows Normally.

    Safe Mode
    Safe Mode with Networking
    Safe Mode with Command Prompt

    Last Known Good Configuration (your most recent settings that worked)

    Start Windows Normally

Use the up and down arrow keys to move the highlight to your choice.
Seconds until Windows starts: 29

Last Known Good Configuration option
Figure 8-3

3. Try to repair Windows. The files for your computer's
installation of Windows may have been damaged (in
technical terms, *corrupted*) as the result of a problem with
the hard disk, an electrical spike that got past your surge
protector and into the computer, or a computer virus (see
Chapter 6). For directions on repairing Windows, see
Chapter 14.

4. Reinstall Windows, which essentially refreshes all your
system files and leaves your data and software programs
intact. In the worst-case scenario, you may have to perform a *clean install*, which requires electrically wiping the
disk clean, reformatting it, and installing Windows all
over again. For details, see Chapter 14.

Check and Change Display Settings in Windows XP and Vista

1. Right-click anywhere on the desktop and choose Properties from the shortcut menu, or choose Start⇨Control Panel and double-click the Display icon. The Display Properties dialog box opens.

 Some advanced video adapters add their own control panels to computer systems. You may find some more advanced customization settings in these control panels, as well as diagnostic tools specific to your PC's hardware.

2. Click the Settings tab. You see the screen resolution and color quality that your video adapter is using (see **Figure** 8-4).

Slide to change the display's configuration.

Choose a new setting from this drop-down menu.

Figure 8-4

If your adapter and its drivers are installed properly, the color and resolution settings offer only options that are within the capabilities of your adapter. For the most modern adapters, you may see only Highest (32 Bit) or Medium (16 Bit) options; older adapters may offer settings that identify the number of colors, beginning as low as 16 or 256 and moving on to true color (16 bit for 65KB colors to 32 bit for more than 4 billion colors).

3. Make any changes you want.

4. Click OK to save your changes.

 If you can't check a problem with your video adapter's device driver (see the appropriate section for your version of Windows later in this chapter) or made an error in choosing adapter settings, you're caught in a conundrum — a computer Catch-22. How do you troubleshoot a device when you need to use that device to see the screen? Here's how: Restart your computer in safe mode and then perform the steps in this section. (For the full start-in-safe-mode procedure, flip to Chapter 17.)

Check and Change Display Settings in Windows 7

1. Right-click anywhere on the desktop, and choose Personalize from the shortcut menu. The Personalization window opens (see **Figure 8-5**).

2. Click Display in the bottom-left corner to open the Display screen.

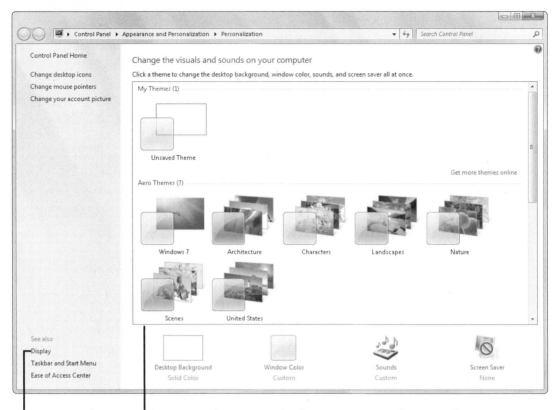

Choose a theme to change multiple settings simultaneously.

Click to access screen resolution and color quality.

Figure 8-5

3. Click Adjust Resolution on the left side of the Display screen. The Screen Resolution screen opens (see **Figure 8-6**).

 You can also access the screen-resolution settings from the shortcut menu when you right-click your desktop.

4. Click the Advanced Settings link to open the Advanced Settings dialog box.

Adjust the slider to set the desired screen resolution.

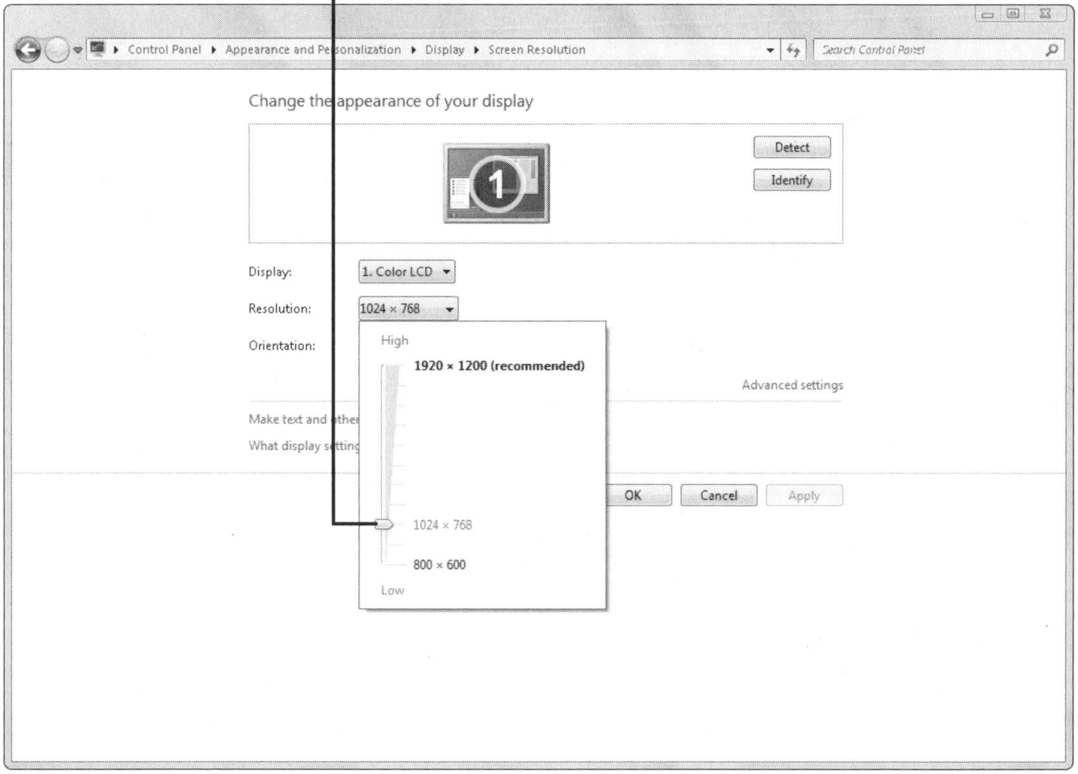

Figure 8-6

5. Click the Monitor tab, and make a choice from the Colors drop-down menu in the bottom-left corner (see **Figure 8-7**).

6. Make any other changes you want.

7. Click OK to save your changes and close the dialog box.

8. Close both of the windows.

Choose color settings.

Figure 8-7

Troubleshoot a Video Adapter in Windows XP and Vista

1. Choose Start⟹Control Panel, and double-click the System icon. The System Properties dialog box opens.

2. Click the Hardware tab.

3. Click Device Manager to open Device Manager (see **Figure 8-8**).

4. Click the plus sign (+) next to the Display Adapters listing to expand it. A yellow question mark next to anything indicates possible trouble; a red exclamation mark tells you that you definitely have a problem.

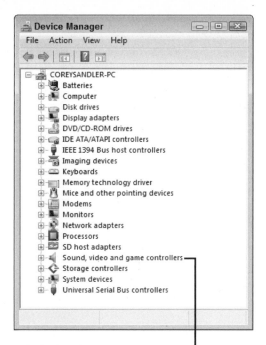

Click this listing to see your PC's video adapters.

Figure 8-8

5. Double-click an adapter to display its Properties dialog box.

6. Click the General tab (see **Figure 8-9**), and check the Device Status box to see whether the system is reporting a problem. If so, click the Troubleshoot button, and follow the onscreen instructions. If not, click OK to close the dialog box.

Any problems will be listed here.

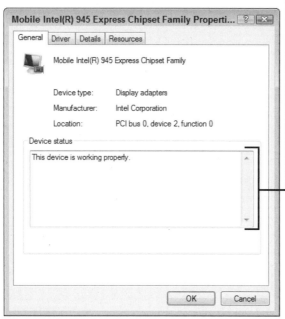

Figure 8-9

Troubleshoot a Video Adapter in Windows 7

1. Choose Start⇨Control Panel, and click Hardware and
Sound to display the Hardware and Sound screen.

2. Click the Device Manager link under the Devices and
Printers heading. Device Manager opens (refer to Figure
8-8, earlier in this chapter).

3. Click the plus sign (+) next to the Display Adapters listing to expand it. A yellow question mark next to anything indicates possible trouble; a red exclamation mark
tells you that you definitely have a problem.

4. Double-click an adapter to display its Properties
dialog box.

5. Click the General tab, and check the Device Status box to see whether the system is reporting a problem. If so, click the Troubleshoot button, and follow the onscreen instructions. If not, click OK to close the dialog box.

Reset a Video Driver

1. Follow the steps in "Troubleshoot a Video Adapter" for your version of Windows, earlier in this chapter, to open the adapter's Properties dialog box.

2. Click the Driver tab to display settings like the ones shown in **Figure 8-10**.

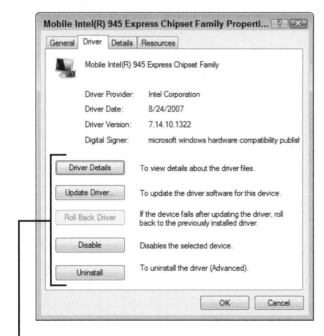

Click these buttons to view and change driver settings.
Figure 8-10

3. Click the appropriate button:

- **Driver Details:** Click to display details about the driver files in use.

- **Update Driver:** Follow the instructions to update the driver from a supplied disc or from a file you've downloaded from the manufacturer's Web site. (See Chapter 4 for more info on updating software.)

- **Roll Back Driver:** If the device fails to operate properly after you install an updated driver, you can choose this option to uninstall the new driver and reinstate the old one.

- **Disable:** Don't click this button unless you have more than one video adapter in your system. With your only video adapter disabled, you wouldn't be able to view your computer's data.

- **Uninstall:** Choose this option to remove the existing driver without installing a replacement.

 A word of existential warning: If you choose the Uninstall option for your default video adapter, you may be unable to view the screen, because the adapter won't be able to communicate with Windows. Restart in safe mode (see Chapter 17), and follow the steps in "Check and Change Display Settings" for your version of Windows, earlier in this chapter, to roll back to the preceding driver or reinstall a driver.

4. Click OK to save your changes and close the dialog box.

Prevent Future Picture Problems

➠ **Reduce the number of open programs or windows.** The more programs you have open, the higher the demand on system resources. Close any programs that aren't necessary.

➠ **Avoid running too many graphics-intensive programs at the same time.** Certain program combinations — a video player and a graphical drawing program running together, for example — may overwhelm your PC and its video adapter. The images you see onscreen may load slowly, skip, or jitter. Again, close any programs that aren't necessary.

➠ **Reduce the display resolution.** In general, the highest resolutions and the highest number of colors in the palette require the most system resources. Try reducing the resolution (see "Check and Change Display Settings" for your version of Windows, earlier in this chapter) to see whether problems go away. If so, consider adding more RAM to the system. Chapter 10 gives you details on installing memory.

Solving Electrical and Mechanical Problems

You can divide a computer's essential vital systems into four areas:

➠ **Electrical:** Electrical power energizes the machine's brain, storage, and other functions.

➠ **Mechanical:** Tiny electrical motors and mechanisms run disks, drives, and fans.

➠ **Electronic:** A collection of circuits centered on a microprocessor manipulates data in a computer.

➠ **Logical:** All the hardware in a computer exists to respond to commands from various types of software, which make up the computer's logical system.

Fixing electronic circuits is far beyond the scope of this book, and software problems are covered in Chapter 4 and in Part IV, which deals with the operating system. So in this chapter, I cover the two remaining types of problems: electrical and mechanical (except for hard drives, which are the subject of Chapter 11). I also briefly mention modems, which can have both electrical and mechanical ailments.

For purposes of this chapter, I'm going to assume that before your computer stopped working, it was running properly.

Diagnose a Failing Power Supply

➠ **Is the electrical outlet supplying current?** Test it with a lamp or radio. If a circuit breaker has shut off current to the outlet, try to determine what caused it to close down. Is another major appliance (such as a refrigerator, large-screen television set, or space heater) using the same circuit?

➠ **Are the computer's fans and drives still running?** If so, that fact may indicate that the power supply is still functioning. On the other hand, if none of the computer's indicator lights, fans, or other electrical parts seems to be alive, the power supply may not be supplying.

➠ **Do you smell anything?** Often, the first sign of impending doom is a whiff of the particular acrid odor of fried electronics; sometimes, the smell precedes the failure.

➠ **Do you hear anything?** Did you hear a pop or sizzle coming from the computer? This auditory clue frequently precedes the olfactory hint that something electrical is shorting out or failing. Turn off power now, and check inside the case to find out what's hot and what's not.

➠ **Do you see anything?** Electrical scorch marks or melted wiring are possible signs of a failure of the power supply.

If you see smoke (or flames), immediately turn off the computer by using the switch on your surge protector or removing the electrical cord from the wall socket. If things don't calm down quickly, call the fire department and head out the door.

Research a Replacement Power Supply

1. Open the case of your PC, following the directions in Chapter 2.

2. Locate the power supply, which is almost always a large metallic box in a corner of the case (see **Figure 9-1**).

Power supply

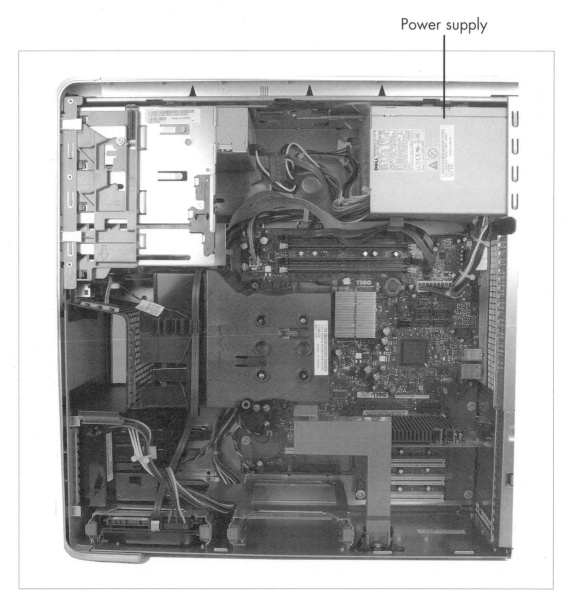

Figure 9-1

You can also look for the point where the electrical cord from the wall current attaches to the computer and follow it to the power supply at the other end, inside the case.

3. Make note of any model information and specifications that you find on the power supply.

4. Write down the details about the power supply's *form factor*, a term that refers to the size and shape of the power supply and the way it bolts to the case. The most common designs for modern computers are

- **ATX:** In this design, a 20-pin connector delivers power to the motherboard, and a separate 4-pin cable and connector together deliver the same set of voltages and control circuits to the microprocessor (see **Figure 9-2**).

- **BTX:** A 24-pin connector goes directly to a 24-pin receptacle on the motherboard. Note, however, that BTX motherboards are fairly rare commodities; few manufacturers converted to this proposed Intel design, and newer, smaller computer circuits pretty much leapfrogged it.

Cables and connectors of an ATX power supply

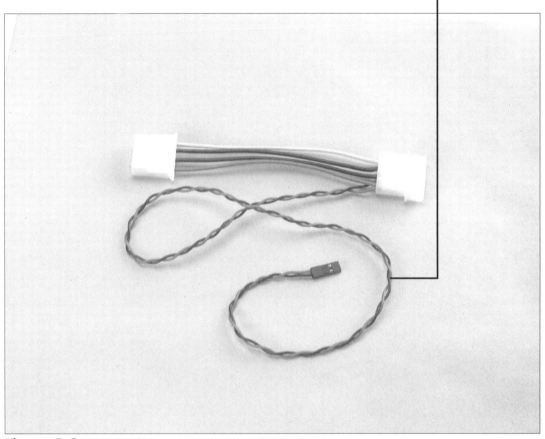

Figure 9-2

5. Check the wattage. The power supply has to produce at
least the minimum amount of wattage to power the
motherboard and everything else attached to the system.
Supplies are usually rated for the amount of continuous
and peak wattage that they can deliver. Look for this
information on the manufacturer's label, like the one
shown in **Figure 9-3**.

Key information about the manufacturer and ratings
usually appear on a label like this one.

Figure 9-3

 Keep in mind the proper thermal fit for your
machine. If you replace a 500-watt power supply
with a 750-watt unit, for example, you need to know
whether your computer is capable of exhausting the
extra heat that the larger unit will produce. Seek guid-
ance from suppliers if necessary.

6. Check the cables and connectors. Make a list of the types
of connectors your computer uses and the number
required of each type. Here's what you have to match:

- **P1 connector:** A modern computer has one main connector from a standard power supply to the motherboard. Designers refer to it as the PC main connector or (as I do) P1. It's the largest and most important of the cables and connectors running from the power supply. Depending on design, a P1 may use a connector with 20 or 24 pins (refer to the descriptions of ATX and BTX designs in Step 4). You can see in **Figure** 9-4 that this connector is very large compared with anything else on the motherboard. You should have no problem finding that connector again if you're reconnecting the existing power supply or installing a new one.

P1 connector attaches here on an ATX motherboard.

Figure 9-4

If you have a really old computer (one that was put into service more than a decade ago), it may use an AT power supply. This design brings power to the motherboard through two separate sets of cables and connectors, labeled P8 and P9 (see **Figure 9-5**).

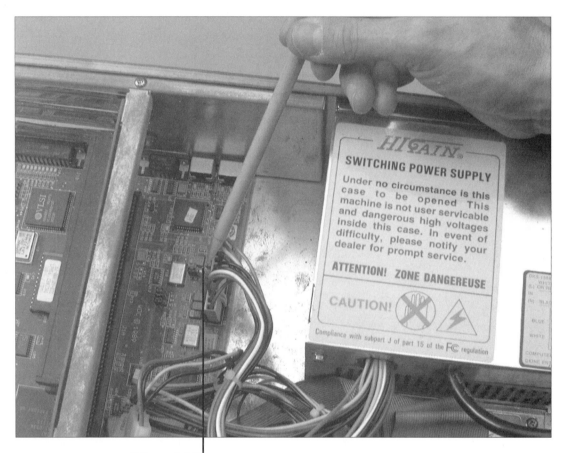

P8 and P9 connectors

Figure 9-5

- **P4 connector:** The superfast microprocessors on modern motherboards are fed by their own source of 12-volt power, delivered through a 4-pin connector labeled P4 (see **Figure 9-6**). Some high-end computers require two P4 connections or a single 8-pin connector.

P4 microprocessor power connector

Figure 9-6

- **Molex connectors:** The next set of connectors coming off the power supply (see **Figure** 9-7) delivers current to peripherals such as hard drives and in some designs to special adapters plugged into the system's electrical bus. The attachment points of these Molex connectors are about an inch long and are fed by four wires — typically, a red wire carrying +5 volts, a yellow wire delivering +12 volts, and two black wires that serve as grounds.

- **Auxiliary power connectors:** Lowest on the electrical totem pole are auxiliary power connectors (see **Figure** 9-8), which are often used to deliver current to tiny fans placed atop particularly hot microprocessors and graphics cards. Some of these small assemblies involve only two wires and a connector the size of a match head.

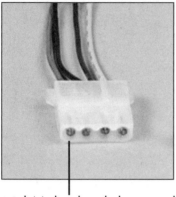

Typical Molex hard drive and
peripheral power connector
Figure 9-7

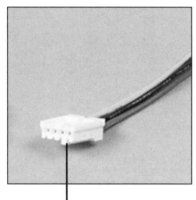

Miniature auxiliary power connector
Figure 9-8

7. With all this information in hand, visit a full-service
computer retailer or online store. A competent salesper-
son or support representative should be able to help you
make the proper match.

Remove and Replace the Power Supply

1. Prepare a well-lit, stable working space. For details on
setting up your working environment and tools, see
Chapter 2.

2. Choose Start➪Shut Down to close Windows and turn off your computer.

3. Unplug the electrical cord that connects the power supply to wall current. Also remove any cables and plugs that attach to ports on the computer if they might interfere with your ability to open the case and work inside.

4. Open the computer's case (see Chapter 2).

5. Carefully examine the placement of the power supply, as well as the wires and connectors that exit it inside the case (see "Research a Replacement Power Supply," earlier in this chapter).

6. To remind yourself what plugs in where, put a piece of masking tape on each connector coming from the power supply, and mark it with a number; then put a piece of tape marked with the same number on the connection point (on the motherboard or an internal device such as a hard drive).

or

With a digital or video camera, take a series of close-up shots of the interior of the computer to help you remember how things looked before you began your surgery.

 Although modern computers are pretty sturdy devices, a large static discharge can still damage delicate components. It's good practice to touch the case with one hand and then touch the motherboard with the other hand. Without removing the hand that's on the motherboard, now you can move the hand that's on the case to the motherboard to help you disconnect the wires.

7. When all the connections have been labeled, photographed, or filmed, unfasten the power cables that attach to the motherboard. Most wires and cables inside the case are held in place by clips along the side of connectors or merely by the friction of a tight fit. Take your time, and be careful: These connectors aren't designed for heavy use, and the motherboard itself can be fragile.

8. Remove the screws that attach the power supply to the case. In general, you need to use a screwdriver (either a flat-head or an X-shaped Phillips-head tool) to remove these screws. In many designs, all the attachment points are on the outside frame.

 Take great care using any metal tool inside the case so that you don't scratch the fine electrical traces that carry power between parts on the motherboard. Also, be very careful not to drop any screws into the interior of the case. If any do land there, you must retrieve them before you turn the computer back on; otherwise, they will short out electrical parts.

9. Remove the power supply itself.

10. To install the new power supply, perform Steps 9–3 in reverse order. Make sure that you correctly reinstall the power connectors to the motherboard and all other internal parts.

Replace the Cooling Fan

1. Prepare a well-lit, stable working space. For details on setting up your working environment and tools, see Chapter 2.

2. Choose Start⇨Shut Down to close Windows and turn off your computer.

3. Unplug the electrical cord that connects the power supply to wall current. Also remove any cables and plugs that attach to ports on the computer if they might interfere with your ability to open the case and work inside.

Figure 9-9 shows the back of a computer case with an auxiliary fan below the power supply fan.

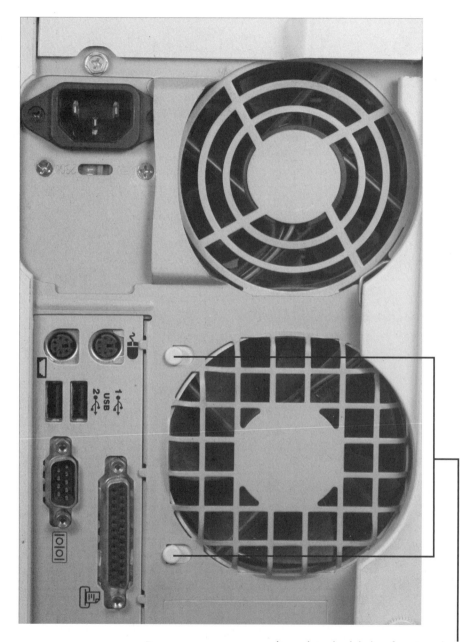

Remove screws or clips that hold the fan in place.

Figure 9-9

4. Open the case (see Chapter 2).

5. Locate the malfunctioning fan. There usually is a fan mounted on the back of the case or sometimes on the front toward the bottom of the case. You may also see a fan on top of the motherboard or mounted directly on top of the microprocessor.

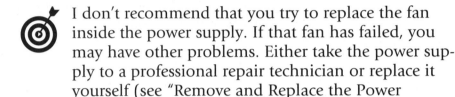 I don't recommend that you try to replace the fan inside the power supply. If that fan has failed, you may have other problems. Either take the power supply to a professional repair technician or replace it yourself (see "Remove and Replace the Power Supply," earlier in this chapter).

6. Locate the power cord, trace it back to the accessory plug, and unplug it.

7. Remove the mounting screws (or sometimes just sliders or snaps) that hold the fan in place (see **Figure 9-10**). A motherboard-mounted fan may sit in a board expansion slot; a microprocessor fan just snaps to the top of the chip's heat sink or carrier.

8. Lift the fan out of the case.

9. To install the new fan, perform Steps 8–3 in reverse order.

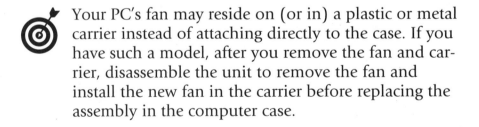 Your PC's fan may reside on (or in) a plastic or metal carrier instead of attaching directly to the case. If you have such a model, after you remove the fan and carrier, disassemble the unit to remove the fan and install the new fan in the carrier before replacing the assembly in the computer case.

Remove screws or clips that hold the fan in place.

Figure 9-10

Mend a Modem

1. Make sure that the modem is receiving electrical power. If not, plug it into an active electrical outlet.

2. Check the indicator lights to see whether the modem is connected to a live signal from the company that provides your Internet service. Any flashing red or yellow lights may indicate a problem with the signal. **Figure 9-11** shows an integrated cable modem, wireless access point, and voice gateway with all lights green except the wireless lamp at the bottom.

Check the modem lights for network and Internet connection status.

Figure 9-11

If you have a cable modem and cable television service, check to see whether any TV set on the premises is receiving a picture. If the TV screen is blank, the problem lies somewhere between the cable company and the modem. It could be that the local system is out of service for the moment, a repair crew is working somewhere in your neighborhood, or the wiring in your home or office is damaged. Call the cable company's technical support number, and ask a support representative to check for problems.

3. Make sure that you have proper connections between the modem and your computer.

4. If the modem has electrical power, a live signal, and correct connections but still isn't working, try doing a power-off reset of your modem. Some models have an actual on/off switch; you turn off others by unplugging them. Leave the modem off for about 15 seconds and then reapply the power.

 If everything seems to check out at your end, call your ISP's support department. Someone there can log in to your modem, test the settings, and probably get things working again if you don't have hardware issues.

Installing Memory

*O*ne of the most basic — and not terribly complex — operations you can perform inside the case of your computer involves installing system memory modules, or RAM (which stands for *random-access memory*). No soldering or arc-welding is involved, and the lifting is very light. You just have to pay close attention to details and take care not to damage your computer while you try to make it better.

Adding memory (up to your machine's specific limit) is generally the most cost-efficient way to increase its speed. Doubling a modern PC's memory from 1GB to 2GB of RAM may boost overall operation speed by as much as 50 percent; going from 2GB to 4GB could give you a 25 percent improvement. Why the discrepancy? That first jump gives Windows and other programs most of the space they need for efficient operation. Moving from 2GB to 4GB improves performance, but not as much as the first step up does.

In this chapter, I show you the basics on installing memory. For much more information, check out my book *Fix Your Own PC* (Wiley Publishing).

Find the Right Memory Module

 Check the specifications for your computer to find the maximum amount of RAM it's capable of managing. Most modern computers sold to consumers can handle no more than 4GB; paying for and installing more than the maximum is a waste of money and could cause problems in some machines.

To find out what kind of memory modules you already have installed in your PC (and need to purchase), use one of these methods:

➠ Choose Start➪All Programs➪Accessories➪System Tools➪System Information. The System Information window opens, displaying a report on memory (among other things), as shown in **Figure 10-1**.

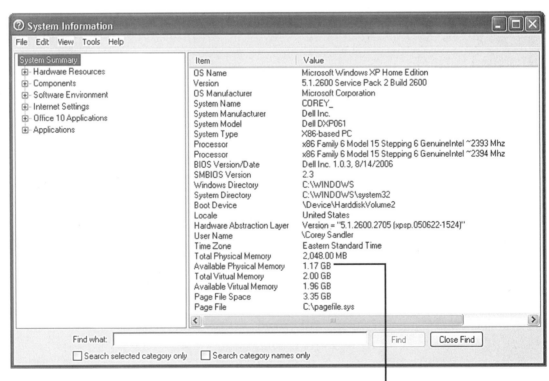

Physical memory is what's installed on physical modules inside your PC.

Figure 10-1

➡ Visit your PC maker's Web site, which may have a feature that will scan your system or tell you what memory was installed at the time of purchase.

➡ Visit a computer retailer's Web site, and look up the parts you need by entering the manufacturer and model number of your computer. The System Information window (refer to Figure 10-1) displays the manufacturer name and model.

➡ Get an online memory scan. Several companies that sell memory modules offer an online scan of your computer that identifies the kind of memory you need. One example is Micron Technology's Crucial System Scanner at www.crucial.com.

Do you really need to know the difference among SDRAM, DDR, DDR2, and DDR3? Not really, except to recognize that these are four of the most common types of memory modules for modern PCs. How about the speed difference between, say, PC2-5200 and PC2-5300? Same thing applies. If your system is designed to use DDR PC2-5200 memory, that's what you should shop for.

Install a New Memory Module

Nearly all memory vendors provide instructions for installing their modules. Many also answer questions over the phone or through a chat feature on their Web sites.

1. Prepare your workspace, assemble your tools, and ground yourself properly (see Chapter 2).

2. Make sure that the computer is turned off, and unplug the power cord and cables.

3. Place the computer on a sturdy, well-lighted surface, and open its case (see Chapter 2).

4. Look for a set of long slots that hold upright DIMM memory modules. Most motherboards have two or four such slots, usually black, with a set of plastic lockdown/ejector clips at each end. The system shown in **Figure 10-2** has a four-slot motherboard.

Installed memory modules, latched into place by clips.

Partly installed memory modules

Figure 10-2

If you've already run a scanning program (see "Find the Right Memory Module," earlier in this chapter), you should know how many DIMM slots to look for and how many of them are already filled. In general, you should have two or four identical modules. If you are installing larger or faster modules as a pair, they should go in the first two slots. In most designs, the slots closest to the microprocessor are considered to be slots 0 and 1 (and are marked that way on the motherboard in tiny letters).

 I mention SDRAM (Synchronous Dynamic Random Access Memory), DDR (Double Data Rate), and other memory types earlier in this section. These terms refer to how the memory chips work. DIMM (Dual Inline Memory Module) refers to how the chips are mounted on a circuit board and installed in your system.

5. If you need to remove an old module to install a new one, press evenly on both of the lockdown/ejector clips to release the unit; then lift the module straight up and out of the slot. Place the removed module on a nonconductive surface such as a cardboard box or plastic bag.

6. Take the new module out of its antistatic bag, holding it by the edges. Avoid touching the metallic connectors on each side of the bottom of the module to keep oils from your fingers from interfering with the module's contact with the motherboard.

7. Follow the installation instructions provided by the memory seller. In most situations, you'll be asked to put the largest-capacity modules in the first slots and the smaller ones in the higher-numbered slots; for a small number of motherboards, you'll be asked to do things the other way around.

8. Locate the notch in the row of pins at the bottom of the module. It needs to line up with a matching pin or key in the DIMM slot on your motherboard (see **Figure 10-3**). The location of the notch depends on the type of module your computer uses.

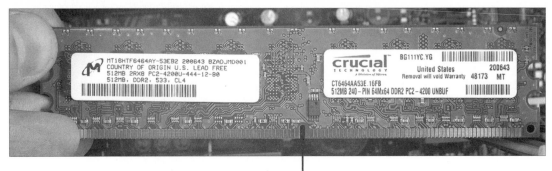

This notch lines up with a pin on the motherboard.

Figure 10-3

 If the notch and pin don't line up, turn the module 180 degrees and try that way.

9. With the notch and pin aligned, press evenly on both ends of the module until it's fully inserted into the slot on the motherboard and the lockdown/ejector clips click into place.

 Don't attempt to force the module into the slot if it seems to be a complete mismatch. Contact the provider of the memory module to make sure that you received the proper type for your PC.

10. Spend a minute or two examining the inside of the case to make sure that all the memory modules are locked down properly and that you didn't leave any tools, pens, or other objects inside.

11. Put the cover back on, secure it properly, and return the machine to its usual location.

12. Reattach the cables and power cord, and turn on the juice.

13. Check the amount of installed memory, which you can do in either of two ways:

- **Watch the startup screen carefully.** Many computers display the amount of installed memory in the startup screen — usually in megabytes, so a bit of translation may be necessary. In computer math, 1,024MB is 1,000 megabytes, which is the same as 1 gigabyte (1GB). So if you put 4GB of memory in your machine, you may see it displayed as 4,096MB.

- **Check the System Information dialog box.** To open this dialog box, refer to "Find the Right Memory Module," earlier in this chapter.

Troubleshoot Jumbled Memory

So what do you do if your computer doesn't recognize the new memory or refuses to start up after you install a new module?

➠ If the computer starts but displays an error message during startup, read the details of the message carefully. Some computers may detect new memory and then ask you to restart so that the memory settings are updated.

 Some older computers may have BIOS (Basic Input Output System) chips that don't recognize more modern memory modules or larger amounts of memory. See the next paragraph for details on what to do.

➠ If your computer starts after the installation of new modules but reports an incorrect amount of RAM, perform the troubleshooting steps at the end of this section to make certain that the new units are installed properly. If the problem continues, check with the maker of your machine to see whether a BIOS update is available. In most cases, the update can be delivered to you over the Internet.

➠ If the computer won't start, first make sure that you reconnected the power cords and other cables to your PC after installing memory.

➠ If all the connections are in place but the computer still won't start, reopen the case (see Steps 1–3 of "Install a New Memory Module," earlier in this chapter) and then follow these steps:

1. Go back to the start of the installation instructions, and recheck each step.

2. Make certain that the modules are fully seated in their slots, with the lockdown/ejector clips latched into place at both ends.

3. Remove the modules (see Step 5 of "Install a New Memory Module," earlier in this chapter), and examine them carefully (see **Figure 10-4**). Make sure that the notches in the modules line up with the pins in the motherboard slots and then reinstall them.

4. Look around inside your computer to make sure that you haven't accidentally disconnected one of the internal power cables to the hard drive or other components.

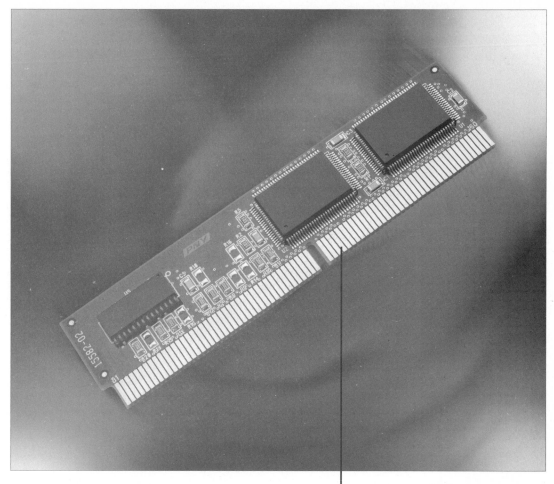

Carefully remove the newly installed modules and re-install them.

Figure 10-4

5. If you tried all these troubleshooting steps and still can't bring your computer to life or get it to recognize new memory, return the computer to the condition it was in before you put in new modules (see Chapter 16), reinstall the original modules, and then test the PC.

6. If the computer works with the old memory but not with the new memory, contact the seller of the RAM module. You may have purchased the wrong type, or you may be the unlucky owner of a defective module. Manufacturers usually test memory modules, so failure is rare, but it's possible.

Changing a Drive, Made Easy

Chapter 11

*W*hy replace a hard drive? I can give you two very good reasons:

➠ **Cost:** If a hard drive fails, it has to be replaced, because there's no cost-efficient way to repair it.

➠ **Performance:** The other reason to change a hard drive is to increase your computer's efficiency or capacity. A larger hard drive not only gives you more storage space, but also lets Windows use more virtual memory for faster operation.

If you're considering installing a new hard drive because the old one has run out of space, a quick and easy solution is an external drive. You can buy one almost anywhere: a computer supply store, a discount superstore, an electronics shop, or one of thousands of online outlets. Just plug the drive into a USB port or a network switch, and it's ready to go. If your current hard drive still works (and isn't too old), you can add a second drive without having to reinstall Windows and all your applications.

In this chapter, I help you with what some people consider to be the "hard" parts of adding or replacing a drive, but as you'll see, the process isn't too difficult.

For much more detail on hard drives and installation procedures, see my book *Fix Your Own PC* (Wiley Publishing).

Determine What You Need

1. **Will you be installing a new *boot drive* — the one your computer starts from — or an additional drive to use for storage?** On most PCs, the boot drive is connected to the first data port on the motherboard. (By techie tradition, the first port is marked 0, the second is 1, and so on.) There's no difference in the construction of boot and storage drives, but if you're installing a boot drive, you'll have to instruct your computer where to look for Windows and the essential tracks it uses to bring itself to life (see "Format the Drive," later in this chapter).

2. **What kind of data cables does your hard drive use?** Nearly all current PCs use a variation on the *ATA* (Advanced Technology Attachment) design called either *PATA* or *SATA:*

- **PATA (parallel ATA):** Until about 2007, ATA used a wide, flat ribbon cable carrying 40 wires (see **Figure 11-1**), and the 16 bits of each computer word moved along the cable in *parallel* — one alongside another — from the motherboard to the drive, or vice versa.

- **SATA (serial ATA):** Today, most PCs have switched to a thin round cable with just eight wires (see **Figure 11-2**), and the bits of information move along the cable in *serial* communication, with one bit behind another. In addition, the changeover to thin round cables reduces much of the clutter under the covers of a modern PC and improves the flow of cooling air inside the box.

Older computers use a wide ribbon cable for hard drive data.

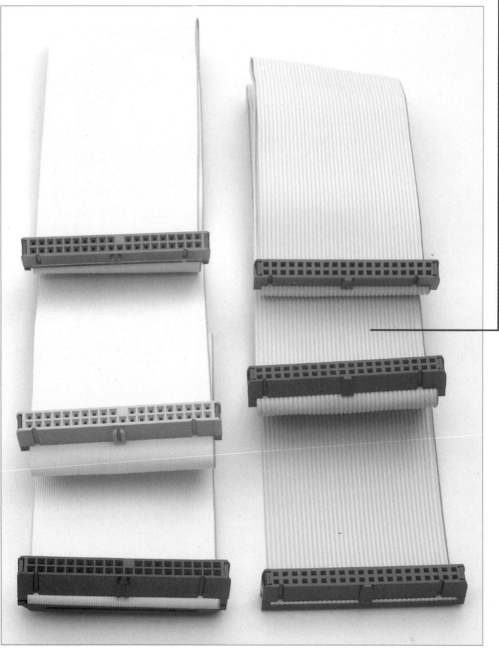

Figure 11-1

Most new machines use the compact serial wire.

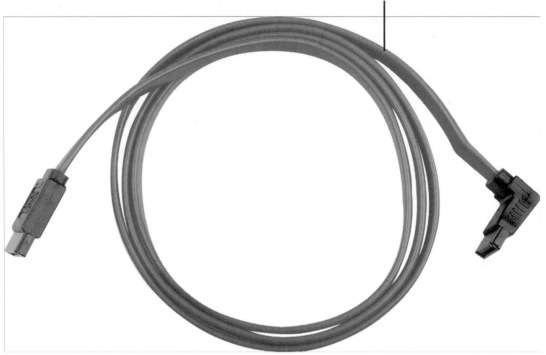

Figure 11-2

3. What attachment points are available?

- **Internal drives:** Some computers have a cage with
  rails like the side ribs of an oven; a hard drive
  slides into the cage along the rails and then is
  secured by screws or latches (see **Figure 11-3**).
  Other computers have multiple slots or rails along
  the frame of the case (see **Figure 11-4**).

 Generally, it doesn't matter where in the case a hard
disk drive is located, because (unlike a CD or DVD
drive) it doesn't provide external access. You do need

to secure the drive, however, so that it doesn't fall on other parts inside the case. Also make sure that it doesn't block the flow of air inside the computer.

- **External drives:** Between the PC and the external drive is a communication cable that plugs into each device. Most external drives also require connection to an electrical outlet, although a few devices can draw their power from the PC through a USB or FireWire cable (see "Install a New External Drive," later in this chapter).

Slide the hard drive into the cage.

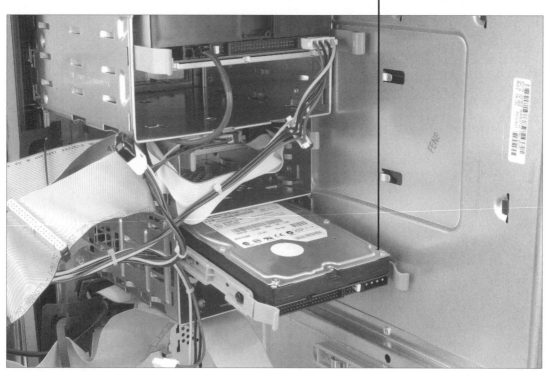

Figure 11-3

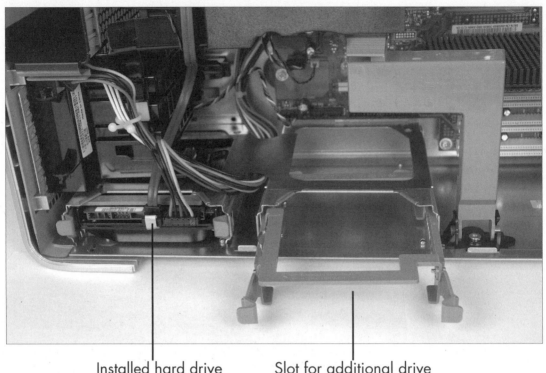

Installed hard drive   Slot for additional drive

Figure 11-4

4. **What type of power-supply connector does the disk drive use?** The computer's power supply (see Chapter 9) provides DC voltage to spin the drive's internal platters, move the read/write head back and forth, and communicate with the computer itself. Your hard drive may use one of the following kinds of cables to connect to the power supply:

> • **Molex connector:** Older PATA drives generally use a large, fat white Molex connector (see **Figure 11-5**). A key on the male connector mates with a slot on the female receptacle on the drive, making it difficult (but not impossible) to install the cable upside down.

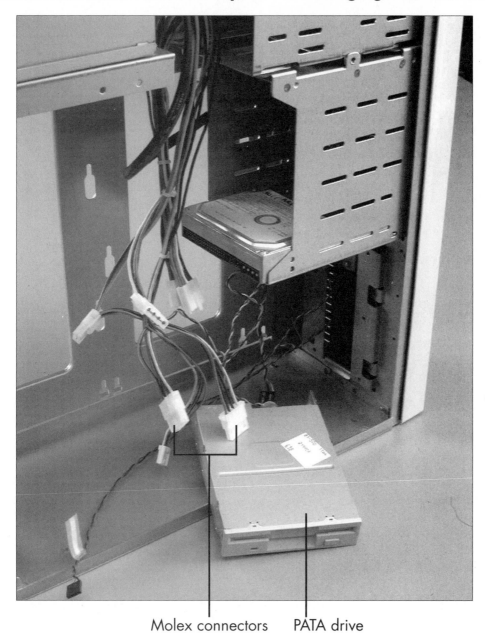

Molex connectors   PATA drive

Figure 11-5

- **SATA connector:** Newer SATA drives use a thin black connector (see **Figure 11-6**) that provides added protection against accidents during installation. Some SATA drives also include a Molex connector as a backup.

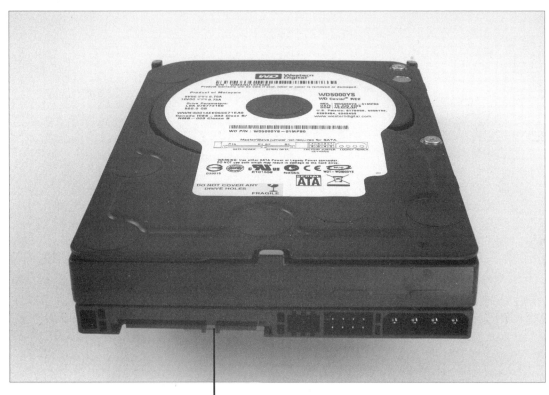

SATA cable connector

Figure 11-6

 You can use a converter to change a Molex connector in your motherboard to a connector that will fit into a SATA receptacle. Just search the Internet for *PATA to SATA adapter*. You'll find many sources, including www.TigerDirect.com and www.satacables.com.

Install a New Internal Drive

1. Prepare your workspace, assemble your tools, and ground yourself properly (see Chapter 2).

 If you're replacing your boot drive, make sure to back up any data that you want to save and install on your new hard drive.

2. Make sure that the computer is turned off, and unplug the power cord and cables.

3. Place the computer on a sturdy, well-lighted surface, and open its case (see Chapter 2).

4. If you're replacing a drive, unplug its data and power cables, and remove it from the case. This process may be as simple as sliding the drive out of a cage. In other cases, you have to remove two or four screws on the sides of the drive. (Put the screws aside so that you can use them with the new drive.)

5. If your new drive needs rails to mount in the case, remove the rails from the drive you took out before installing the rails that should have come with the new drive.

6. Slide the new drive partway into the slot you just vacated or, if you're adding a second drive, partway into a vacant slot. Installing the drive only partway holds it in place but gives you flexibility while you hook up the data and power cables (see Steps 7–8). You'll seat the drive in the slot later.

 Depending on the design of your computer, it may be easier to connect the data and power cables before you slide the drive into place.

7. Find an available data cable and connector near the location where you'll be installing the new drive, and plug this cable into the data port of your new hard drive. Data cables are just lying around inside the case, connected to the motherboard on one end and to nothing or to another hard drive on the other.

Most PATA ribbon cables can connect to two devices, with one device marked *master* and the other marked *slave.* (If you're using a PATA system, consult the drive maker's instructions to find out how to configure the tiny jumpers or switches on the device to match its status as master or slave.) On the other hand, SATA data cables are one to a customer, connecting one device to one interface on the motherboard.

 If the new drive is going to be your boot drive, you generally need to use the first data connector, which usually is marked 0 on the motherboard. If the drive will be used as an additional storage device, you can attach it to any other available data connector.

8. Locate an appropriate power cable, again choosing one near where the new drive will be installed, and plug this cable into the power connector on the new hard drive.

9. Slide the drive into place (see **Figure 11-7**).

10. Make sure that the drive and cables are properly secured and that you didn't leave any tools or other objects inside the case.

11. Put the case back on, secure it, and return the computer to its usual location.

Front-of-case slot for SATA drive

Figure 11-7

12. Reattach the cables and power cord, and turn on the computer.

13. Skip to "Partition the Drive," later in this chapter.

Install a New External Drive

 Most external drives connect to a computer's USB port, so I cover that type in this section. For details on installing a different type, consult the instruction manual or my book *Fix Your Own PC* (Wiley Publishing).

1. Plug the drive's USB cable into a free USB port on your computer.

 Your PC can be on or off when you plug in a USB device.

2. Plug the other end of the USB cable into the external drive's USB connector (see **Figure 11-8**).

3. Attach the power cord to the drive, and plug it into wall current or — better yet — a surge protector (see Chapter 1).

4. Turn on the power to the external drive (and to your computer, if you turned it off before installing the new drive).

Nearly all devices proceed to install any necessary drivers or utilities automatically when you turn them on. Follow any onscreen instructions.

If Windows or your antivirus software displays a security alert during installation, click Accept or Continue. If you can't get past this warning, you can disable your firewall or other security software (see Chapter 6) before continuing with the installation.

5. Proceed to the next section, "Partition the Drive."

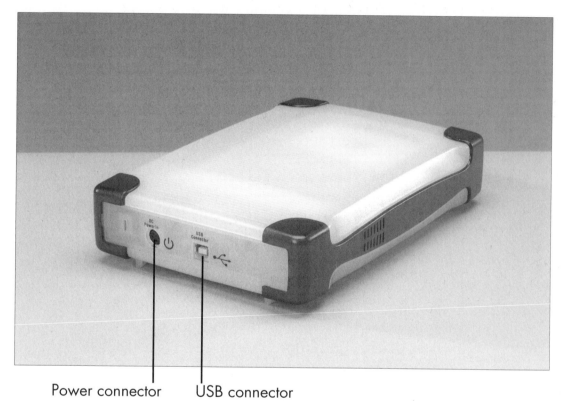

Power connector   USB connector

Figure 11-8

Partition the Drive

The next step in preparing a new disk is *partitioning*, which assigns logical units and file systems to the hard drive. *Partitions* are the basic containers for data. Each partition exists in a specified physical location on the hard drive and functions almost like a separate drive.

1. Decide how many partitions you want to have on your hard drive. Depending on the size of the drive and the version of Windows you're using, you may be able to use a single huge partition. This configuration is the easiest and (in my opinion) best one to use, if your computer supports it. If not, you have to create two or more smaller partitions. A 250GB drive, for example, could be set up as two logical drives of 125GB each, or as one 50GB drive and two 100GB drives.

    Even if your computer can support one large partition, you may want to create at least two partitions. Some professionals recommend creating a relatively small partition — 20MB or so — to hold only Windows and using the rest of the drive for all other programs and data.

2. Use the manufacturer's utility to create the partitions. Hard drive manufacturers usually provide a utility that automates the creation of partitions; this utility (such as the Western Digital example shown in **Figure 11-9**) comes on the drive itself or on an accompanying CD or DVD. Follow the instructions faithfully, and accept the utility's recommendations on what partitions to create.

    Most external drives come preformatted and ready to run immediately in Windows. For information on reformatting, see the next section, "Format the Drive."

Follow the utility's instructions to partition your new drive.

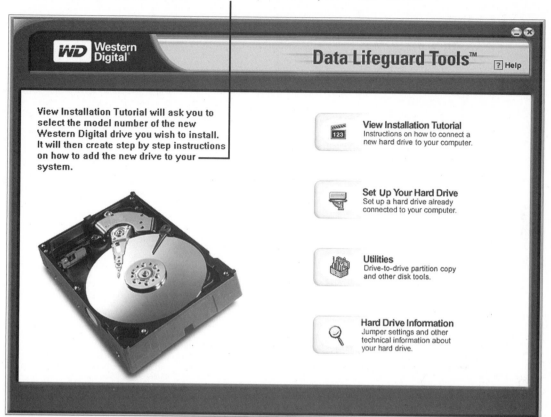

Figure 11-9

Format the Drive

Formatting a drive applies a set of magnetic markers to the disk platters, allowing your computer to set up a file system that indexes what data is placed where.

1. Use the formatting utility included with the hard drive (such as the example shown in **Figure 11-10**) to format the device. For most users, the best practice is to accept the manufacturer's recommended (default) settings. The program may create one of the following types of file systems:

Make any required changes
before you start the process.

Figure 11-10

- **FAT (File Attribute Table):** You would use FAT or FAT32 (see the next paragraph) only if you need to maintain compatibility with older equipment or if you intend to load and switch between a current version of Windows (XP, Vista, or 7) and an older one (such as Windows 95, 98, or ME). That situation isn't likely to apply to most readers of this book.

- **FAT32:** Like FAT, FAT32 is an older file system. Generally, it's unable to deal with drives (or partitions within drives) larger than 32GB.

- **NTFS (Windows NT File System):** If you're using Windows XP, Vista, or 7, the preferred file system is NTFS, which is more efficient than FAT and FAT32, and also more capable of recovering from certain types of disk errors. NTFS is essential for use with large disk drives.

On most new external drives, the standard setup provides a single FAT32 partition, which means that Windows will use the entire capacity of the new drive as a single volume. If you choose to repartition the drive so that it appears to Windows to be two or more drives, you can do so — but doing so will erase any preloaded software or utilities that came with the drive.

2. If you intend to use the new hard drive as your boot drive, install special boot tracks and Windows itself on that drive. You accomplish this task by using a utility provided with the operating system. In most instances, you turn off your computer, place the Windows DVD in your CD/DVD drive, and then turn the computer on again. The computer recognizes the presence of the DVD and gives you the option of installing the operating system on your hard disk drive (see **Figure 11-11**).

Follow the instructions carefully, and be prepared for a lengthy process; most installations require several hours to complete.

Early PCs had one or two floppy disk drives, which were called A and B. To maintain compatibility with older hardware and software, those two letters are not available to identify hard drives in a standard setup. Drive C usually is the boot drive, followed by drives D through Z. (Special utilities are available for rare and unusual configurations with dozens of drives, but that topic is well beyond the scope of this book.)

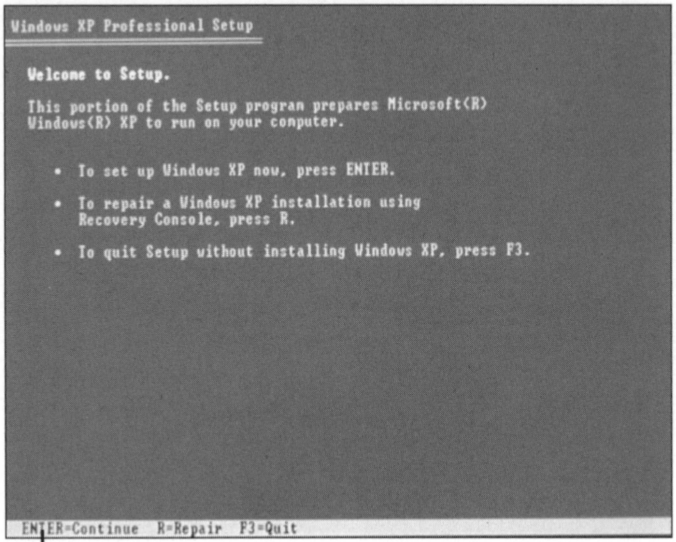

Press Enter to start a new Windows installation.
Figure 11-11

Troubleshoot a New Internal Drive

1. Make sure that you've connected the PATA or SATA data cable securely to the proper port on the motherboard, as described in "Install a New Internal Drive," earlier in this chapter. (For a refresher on the cables themselves, see "Determine What You Need," earlier in this chapter.)

2. Check the power-cable connection (also described in "Install a New Internal Drive," earlier in this chapter).

3. Open the case (see Chapter 2), plug in the PC's power cord, and turn the computer on. Listen for hard drive activity (you should hear the heads moving on an active drive), and check the disk activity light on the front of the case. If the power supply or other internal electronics may have failed; contact the manufacturer for advice on a possible repair.

4. Open Device Manager (see Chapter 18), or open the My Computer or Computer window, as follows:

- **Windows XP:** Choose Start⇨My Computer.

- **Vista and Windows 7:** Choose Start⇨Computer.

The easiest way to access Device Manager in Vista and Windows 7 is to click the Start button and then type **device manager** in the Search Programs and Files text box.

5. View the Disk Drives list. If the drive is in the list, you can double-click it to display a Properties dialog box like the one shown in **Figure 11-12**.

Click the tabs to review hardware and driver status.

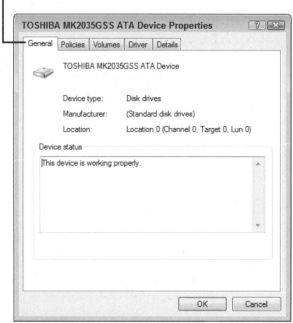

Figure 11-12

6. If the drive doesn't show up in the Computer/My Computer window or in Device Manager, it's not communicating with the computer. Recheck all cables.

7. If the drive still doesn't respond or appear in the My Computer/Computer window or in Device Manager, call the manufacturer for technical support.

Troubleshoot a New External Drive

1. Make sure that the external drive is plugged into a live electrical outlet, turned on, and receiving power. Nearly all external drives use an adapter that transforms AC wall voltage to DC voltage; check to see that all plugs are seated properly in their receptacles.

2. Listen for any activity. I have yet to find a completely silent disk drive. You should be able to hear the drive motor, an internal cooling fan, or both. If the device is switched on and receiving power, but you detect no signs of life, the new drive's power supply or other internal electronics may have failed. Contact the manufacturer for advice on a possible repair.

3. Open Device Manager (see Chapter 18), or open the My Computer or Computer window, as follows:

- **Windows XP:** Choose Start⇨My Computer.

- **Vista and Windows 7:** Choose Start⇨Computer.

 The easiest way to access Device Manager in Vista and Windows 7 is to click the Start button and then type **device manager** in the Search Programs and Files text box.

4. Pull down the Disk Drives list to see whether the new drive is displayed.

5. If the drive doesn't show up in the Computer/My Computer window or in Device Manager, it's not communicating with the computer. Recheck all cables.

6. If the drive still doesn't respond or appear in the My Computer/Computer window or in Device Manager, call the manufacturer for technical support.

7. Try reinstalling the drive's software and device drivers (see Chapter 4).

8. Run a diagnostics program (see Chapter 5) to find out whether the computer's ports are functioning properly. Follow any onscreen instructions.

9. Take advantage of the external drive's portability by testing it on another PC. You could try plugging it into a friend's computer to see whether it recognizes the drive, or maybe a local computer repair shop will allow you to make the same test on its equipment. Don't forget to take — and use — the AC adapter and data cable that came with the drive.

Install a New Internal CD/DVD Drive

 You can use either an internal or an external CD/DVD drive. External drives simply plug into your computer, so I discuss installing an internal drive in this section.

1. Prepare your workspace, assemble your tools, and ground yourself properly (see Chapter 2).

2. Make sure that the computer is turned off, and unplug the power cord and cables.

3. Place the computer on a sturdy, well-lighted surface, and open its case (see Chapter 2) after you've grounded yourself.

4. If your new drive needs rails to mount inside the case, install the rails that should have come with it.

5. Prepare the location for the new drive. You probably need to remove a cover on the front of your case where the new drive will go. This cover may snap off and on, or it may be attached by small screws that you'll need to remove. (Put the screws aside so that you can use them to secure the new drive.)

6. Slide the new drive into the mounting slot. Depending on your case design, you may need to slide the new drive in from the front or (more likely) insert the drive from inside the case so that it sits flush with the front of the case.

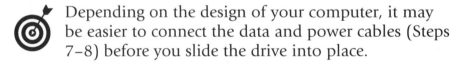 Depending on the design of your computer, it may be easier to connect the data and power cables (Steps 7–8) before you slide the drive into place.

7. Find an available data cable and connector near the location where you'll be installing the new drive, and plug this cable into the data port on your new hard drive (see "Install a New Internal Drive," earlier in this chapter).

8. Locate an appropriate power cable, again choosing one near where the new drive will be installed, and plug it into the power connector on the new drive.

CD and DVD drives provide audio as well as data to your computer. New drives use the data connection for audio only. Check your documentation. If your drive requires an analog audio connection, attach the supplied cable from the drive's audio out to your sound card's audio input connector.

9. Make sure that the drive and cables are properly secured and that you didn't leave any tools or other objects inside the case.

10. Put the case back on, secure it, and return the computer to its usual location.

11. Reattach the cables and power cord, and turn on the computer.

Test a New CD/DVD Drive

1. Open Device Manager (see Chapter 18).

2. Click the plus sign (Windows XP) or the right-facing arrow (Vista and Windows 7) next to the DVD/CD ROM Drives entry.

3. Double-click the DVD/CD drive name in this list to display the Device Properties dialog box (see **Figure 11-13**), and check for the message This device is working properly.

4. (Windows XP only) Click the Properties tab, and make sure that the check box titled Enable Digital CD Audio for This CD-ROM Device is checked.

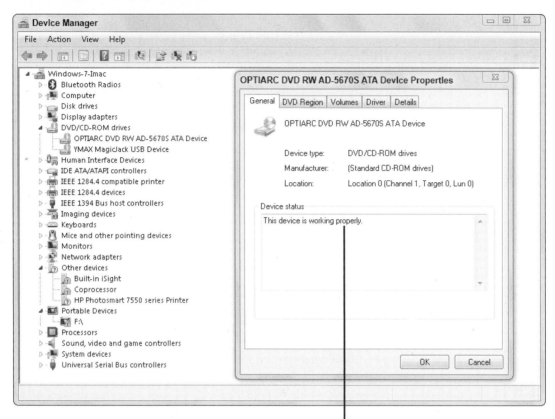

Check whether the new drive is working properly.

Figure 11-13

5. If everything is working properly, click OK to close the Device Properties dialog box. If you don't, follow the troubleshooting steps for your type of drive — internal or external — earlier in this chapter.

6. Install the software that came with the new drive. Windows includes a fairly simple disk-burning application, but your new drive probably includes a more robust program. Install it now according to the manufacturer's instructions.

Fixing a Malfunctioning Printer

You're looking at a beautifully formatted page of text in your word processor or studying an uproarious list of jokes sent by a friend in an e-mail (which, to some people, is the real purpose of the Internet). Or maybe your children have sent some incomparably adorable pictures of your grandchildren. In any case, you want a printed copy to treasure.

You click the Print button in the computer program you're using to get a printout of what you're viewing, and something like this happens:

➠ Nothing happens.

➠ A few lights on the printer flash, but no motors churn.

➠ The printer fires up its engine, begins to load a piece of paper, and then grinds to a stop.

➠ The printer actually prints a page, but you can hardly read it because of light print or skipped characters.

What do you do? In this chapter, I show you some solutions to common printer problems.

Check Printed Pages for Problems

→ **Dark vertical or horizontal lines:** Dark lines running the length or width of a printed page, as you see in **Figure 12-1**, may be caused by a dirty or damaged printhead (inkjet printer), contamination of components (laser printer), or low ink or toner levels (both types). On a laser printer, these lines may also be caused by a scratch or other damage on the drum, which usually is part of the laser cartridge that's replaced when toner is depleted.

→ **Uneven print tones:** If the characters or images on the page are uneven in darkness, that result usually indicates low ink or toner.

 If you're using a laser printer, you can usually eke out a few dozen more pages from a cartridge by removing it and gently shaking it to redistribute the toner.

On a laser printer, other possible causes of uneven printing are damage to the photoreceptor or a light leak into the receptor from a nearby lamp or window. You don't have to operate a laser printer in a darkroom, but you should keep its cover in place except when you have to replace the toner and drum or clear a paper jam. (I keep my laser printer in a corner, away from the windows.)

→ **White vertical lines (laser printers):** White gaps or lines down the page may be caused by damage to the toner cartridge or debris in the path between the cartridge and the drum. You may be able to remove the obstacles; otherwise, you'll have to replace the cartridge.

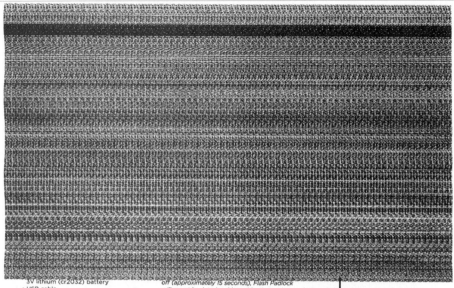

- 3V lithium (cr2032) battery
- USB cable
- Lanyard
- Quick Start Guide (this manual)

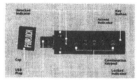

HOW TO OPERATE FLASH PADLOCK
Flash Padlock ships in an unlocked config-uration ready to use in your computer. To enable Flash Padlock's security, you will need to set up a combination. Your combination must be between a minimum of one (1) and a maximum of ten (10) digits.

CAUTION: Once your combination has been set, Flash Padlock will be permanently locked and your data cannot be accessed, unless you enter in your combination. Please store your combination in a safe place, or you may register your combination through secure registration at the Corsair Website: http://www.corsair.com/padlock.

off (approximately 15 seconds), Flash Padlock will revert back to its old combination and you will need to restart the process. If no combination was set, Flash Padlock will revert back to its original unopened status.

Step 5: The GREEN LED will blink to indicate the combination has been set. When the GREEN LED is flashing, Flash Padlock will remain unlocked for about 15 seconds. When the GREEN LED stops flashing, Flash Padlock will Auto-Lock and will require you to enter in your PIN to unlock.
NOTE: Auto-Lock will automatically lock Flash Padlock. This is your way of locking your Flash Padlock drive.

HOW TO UNLOCK FLASH PADLOCK
Step 1: Firmly press and quickly release the KEY button. The RED LED will blink to indicate Flash Padlock is locked, but ready for you to enter your combination. You have about 5 seconds to begin Step 2.
NOTE: If you hold the KEY button down for longer than 2 seconds, you will get an error: GREEN and RED lights alternately blinking.

Step 2: While the RED LED is blinking, enter your combination then firmly press and quickly release the KEY button. During this combination entry stage, the RED and GREEN LED lights will blink in unison. If any of the lights turn off, you will need to repeat Step 1.

Step 3: The GREEN LED will blink to indicate Flash Padlock is unlocked.

Step 4: When you are done, firmly press and quickly release the KEY button.

Step 5: Both the RED and GREEN LED lights will blink. You will then need to re-enter your combination to verify. After entering the combination a second time, press and release the KEY button.
NOTE: If you do not verify your combination before the RED and GREEN LED lights turn off (approximately 15 seconds) Flash Padlock will revert back to its old combination and you will need to restart the process.

Step 6: The GREEN LED light will blink to indicate the combination has been set. When the GREEN LED light stops blinking (approximately 15 seconds), the Auto-Lock feature will enable and Flash Padlock goes into its locked state.

HOW TO LOCK FLASH PADLOCK
Step 1: You cannot lock Flash Padlock while it is plugged into your computer. Disconnect Flash Padlock from your computer.

Step 2: Flash Padlock's Auto-Locking feature will secure the drive in approximately 15 seconds. When the GREEN LED light stops blinking, Auto-Lock has secured the drive.
NOTE: If Flash Padlock does not have a combination set, Auto-Lock cannot enable and the drive will remain open. If you want to have Auto-Lock enabled, see instructions on "how to set a combination".

Continued on next page

If you see this, check for dirt in the printer or a damaged component.
Figure 12-1

⟶ **Black or white blotches:** Blotches of black or white on the paper may indicate contamination of the drum or the fusing roller. The drum isn't easy to clean, but if your cartridge includes a drum, like the one shown in **Figure 12-2**, the problem will be fixed when you replace the cartridge. Most printers include a small brush and sometimes a cleaning solution for the fusing roller. Consult the printer's instruction manual for advice.

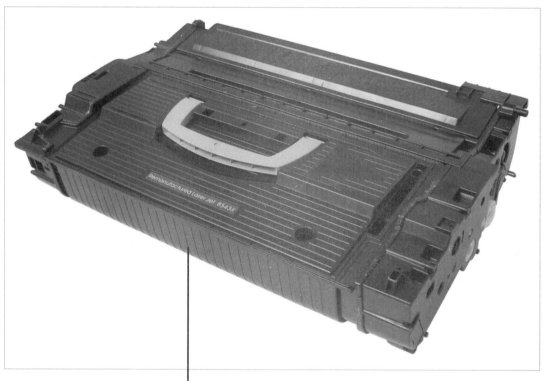

A laser cartridge like this replaces all the critical printer components each time you replace it.

Figure 12-2

⟶ **Streaky lines (laser printers):** Streaks on the page sometimes tell you that toner needs to be cleaned off the printer's rollers or electrostatic parts.

➠ **Low resolution or dropouts (inkjet printers):** The tiny ink nozzles on the print head of an inkjet printer are prone to clogs that can result in loss of resolution or dropouts in text or graphics. Many printers include a utility for cleaning the inkjet head; consult the manual for details.

 One other issue to consider is the quality and type of paper you use in your printer. To get the most out of a laser printer, use good-quality copy paper that's certified for a laser printer or copy machine. Inkjet printers generally require a smoother paper surface because the ink is applied wet, and the text or image can become fuzzy if the ink is absorbed into the paper. Photorealistic inkjet printers work best with glossy or coated stock. Consult the printer manual for advice, and don't be afraid to experiment with small quantities of different paper grades; some office-supply stores offer free sample packs for testing.

Test the Printer's Hardware

1. Make sure that the printer is turned on and plugged into a live electrical outlet. If the printer doesn't seem to have power, test the outlet by plugging in a lamp or radio that you know is working properly. If the lamp lights or the radio sings but the printer won't come to life, the printer may have suffered an electrical failure.

2. Check the printer's paper and ink levels. Some printers are smart enough to stop the job when you run out of supplies but not communicative enough to tell you why. Study the printer's instruction manual to find the meaning of any error lights on the printer or messages on your PC's monitor.

Many — probably most — printers today include software that notifies your Windows printer driver when ink supplies are low. Get into the habit of checking your printer's window each time you send a document to it, and look for a low-ink warning. Click this warning to find out which cartridge will need to be replaced soon.

3. Check for a paper jam. Paper jams are usually caused by one of three conditions:

- **Debris stuck in the paper path:** Consult the instruction manual for advice on cleaning the paper path. Use a vacuum cleaner with a soft brush to remove debris (including tiny pieces of paper).

- **High humidity:** Humidity causes paper to stick to other pieces of paper or to printer rollers.

 One way to deal with humidity is to store your paper in a sealed box, installing only as much as you need to print a job.

- **Inappropriate paper:** Check your printer's specifications for acceptable weights and grades of paper. Stock that's too thin, thick, or glossy can jam a printer. (Also see "Check Printed Pages for Problems," earlier in this chapter.)

4. Run the printer's built-in self-test. Consult the manual or call the manufacturer to find out how to test the machine.

- **If the self-test fails,** and the test program makes no suggestions about repairs (such as cleaning certain parts or replacing ink or toner cartridges), the printer may need servicing at a professional repair shop.

If your printer needs servicing, but its warranty has expired, replacing it probably makes more economic sense than repairing it.

• **If the self-test works,** move on to the next step.

5. Print a test page. To send the test page, turn on the printer and follow these steps:

a. Choose Start⇨Control Panel⇨Printers and Faxes (Windows XP), Start⇨Settings⇨Printers (Vista), or Start⇨Devices and Printers (Windows 7).

b. Right-click the printer's icon, and choose Properties (XP and Vista) or Printer Properties (Windows 7) from the shortcut menu. The printer's Properties dialog box opens (see **Figure 12-3**).

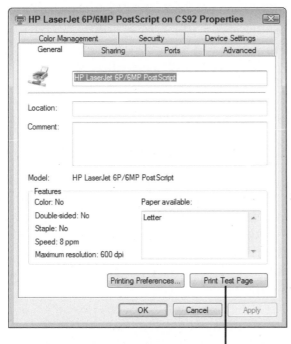

Click Print Test Page to eliminate a particular application as the problem.

Figure 12-3

    c. On the General tab, click the Print Test Page button. Windows displays a message confirming that the test page was sent.

- **If the test page prints successfully,** as shown in **Figure 12-4**, your problem is most likely a setting within a program, such as your word processor. Try resetting the program's printer options.

- **If the test page doesn't print,** click the Troubleshoot Printer Problems link in the test-page confirmation message. The resulting help screen (see **Figure 12-5**) presents the most likely problems and helps you find the support Web site for your particular brand of printer. Click the most appropriate link for your problem. If you don't see your problem listed, click Show All to see a page of other possibilities, including issues with device drivers and *spoolers* (features that store print jobs on the hard drive temporarily while the printer processes other jobs).

6. Switch printer cables. Substitute a data cable that you know to be good, and print a test page again. If the printer works, the original cable has failed and should be replaced.

7. Connect the printer cable to a different USB port. Most computers have at least four and sometimes eight USB ports, and on rare occasions, one may go out of order. To test the port you use to connect to the printer, plug in another device (such as an external disk drive, a flash memory key, or a digital camera) to see whether the system recognizes its presence.

8. Check Device Manager to see whether it's reporting any hardware failures or indicating a problem with any port or printer drivers. For details on using Device Manager, see Chapter 18.

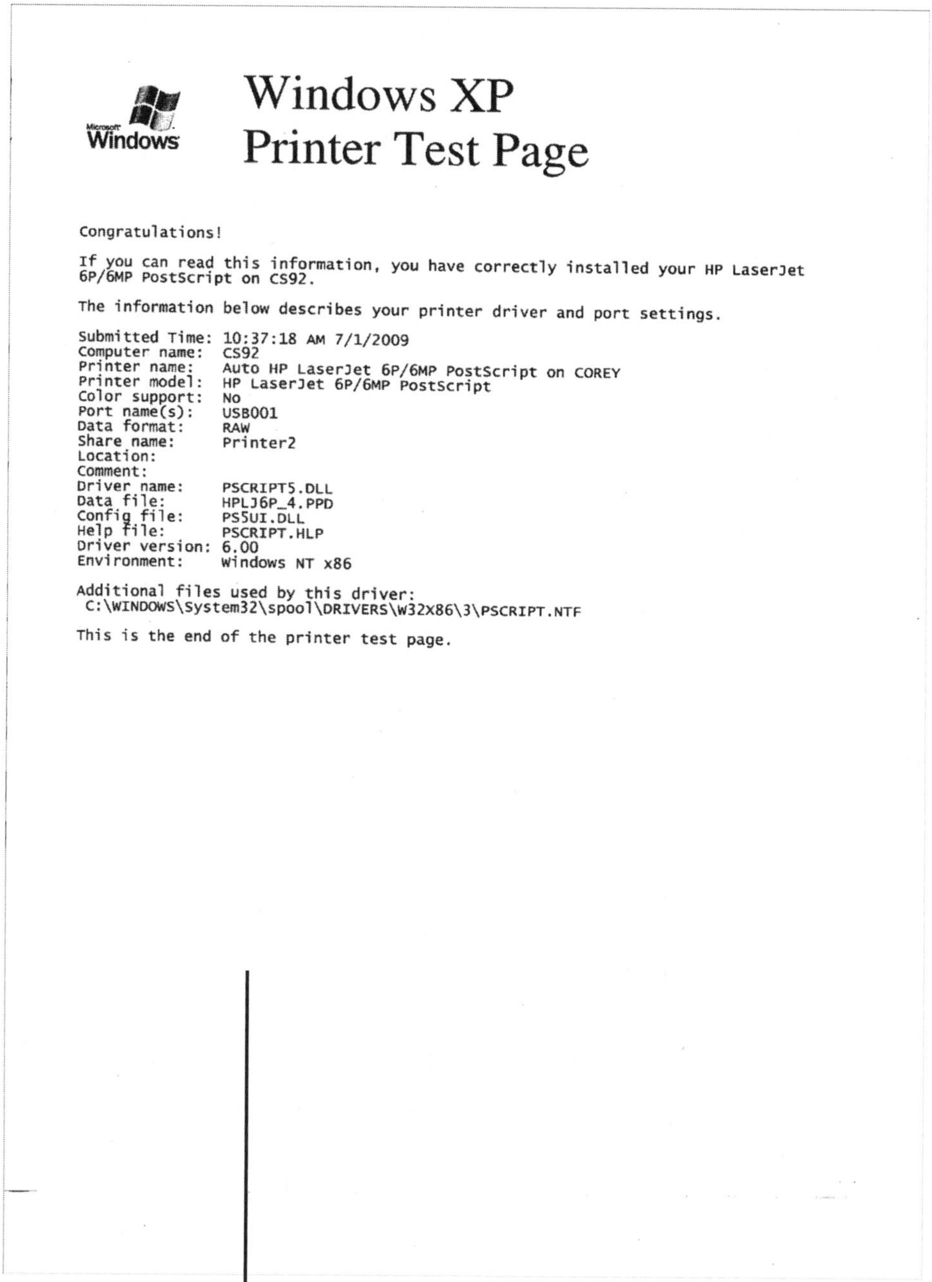

 # Windows XP Printer Test Page

Congratulations!

If you can read this information, you have correctly installed your HP LaserJet 6P/6MP PostScript on CS92.

The information below describes your printer driver and port settings.

```
Submitted Time:  10:37:18 AM 7/1/2009
Computer name:   CS92
Printer name:    Auto HP LaserJet 6P/6MP PostScript on COREY
Printer model:   HP LaserJet 6P/6MP PostScript
Color support:   No
Port name(s):    USB001
Data format:     RAW
Share name:      Printer2
Location:
Comment:
Driver name:     PSCRIPT5.DLL
Data file:       HPLJ6P_4.PPD
Config file:     PS5UI.DLL
Help file:       PSCRIPT.HLP
Driver version:  6.00
Environment:     Windows NT x86
```

Additional files used by this driver:
 C:\WINDOWS\System32\spool\DRIVERS\W32X86\3\PSCRIPT.NTF

This is the end of the printer test page.

Result of a successful test

Figure 12-4

Click to show all

Links to help pages on common printer problems

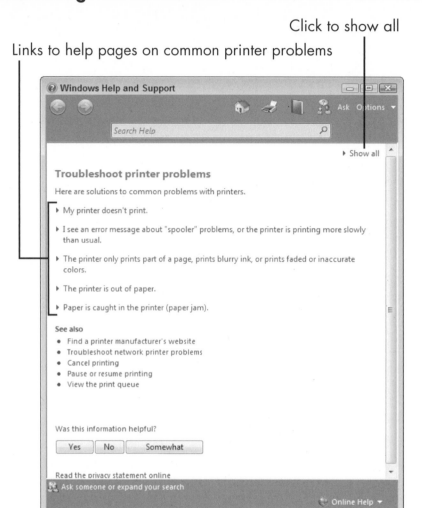

Figure 12-5

9. Hook the printer up to another computer that you know is working properly. You may be able to use a friend's or neighbor's PC. Alternatively, some computer stores may let you bring in your printer to run this test in the hope that you'll end up buying something.

Test the Printer's Software

1. Make sure that you're using the appropriate printer driver and that it's in good condition. A printer's built-in intelligence can freeze or produce garbled output if you use an incorrect, outdated, or corrupted printer driver. To check, follow these steps:

   a. Choose Start⇨Control Panel⇨Printers and Faxes (XP), Start⇨Settings⇨Printers (Vista), or Start⇨Devices and Printers (Windows 7).

   b. Right-click the printer's icon, and choose Properties (XP and Vista) or Printer Properties (Windows 7) from the shortcut menu. The printer's Properties dialog box opens.

   c. Click the Advanced tab (see **Figure 12-6**), and make sure that the driver settings are correct and that the appropriate driver is being used. The driver name should match the brand and model of your printer. If it doesn't match, you could somehow have installed the wrong driver; even if it does match, you can try installing a new driver. To do so, click the New Driver button, and follow the printer wizard's instructions.

2. See whether your printer has enough memory by printing a complex document. If the document doesn't print or is of unacceptable quality, you may need to add more memory to your printer or adjust printer settings to minimize the amount of memory that the document requires. Consult the instruction manual for specifics on adjusting these settings.

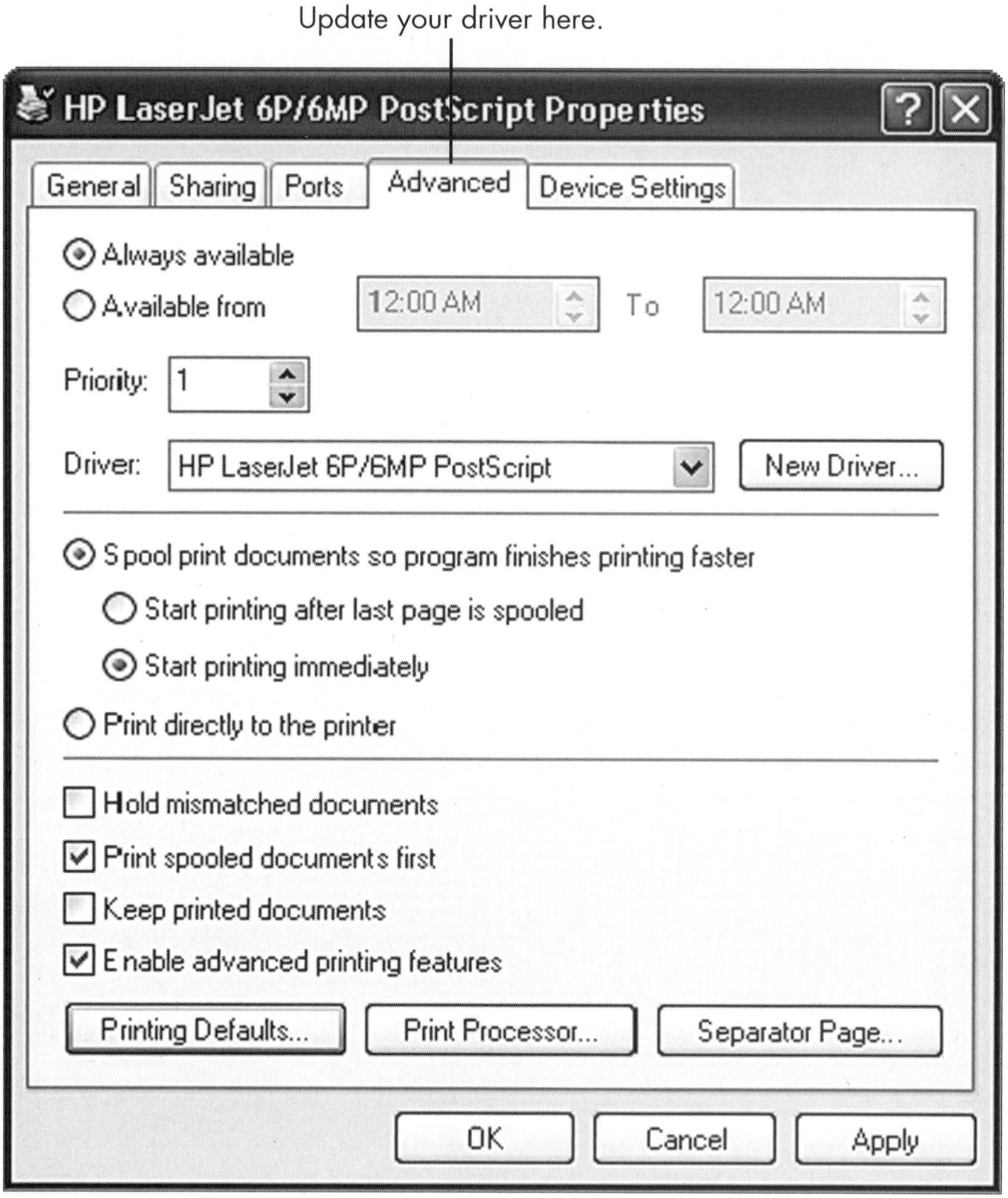
Update your driver here.
HP LaserJet 6P/6MP PostScript Properties
General
Sharing
Ports
Advanced
Device Settings
Always available
Available from
12:00 AM
To
12:00 AM
Priority:
1
Driver:
HP LaserJet 6P/6MP PostScript
New Driver...
Spool print documents so program finishes printing faster
Start printing after last page is spooled
Start printing immediately
Print directly to the printer
Hold mismatched documents
Print spooled documents first
Keep printed documents
Enable advanced printing features
Printing Defaults...
Print Processor...
Separator Page...
OK
Cancel
Apply

Figure 12-6

Taking Care of Your Mouse (or Trackball) and Keyboard

*T*he good news is that mice, trackballs, and keyboards make computing easy. The bad news is that because they're mechanical, they eventually wear out. How people use them affects their life span too. Some users treat the devices gently; others have a clicking and typing style that closely resembles a worker on a chain gang pounding rocks.

You can do a few things to improve the performance of these devices and perhaps extend their lives. Attempting to repair broken units may not make sense, however, because they're so inexpensive. Replacement keyboards, for example, sell for as little as $10.

The *really* good news is that new mice, trackballs, and keyboards are truly "plug and play" devices. Removing the one that came with your computer and replacing it with a new one takes about as much effort and technical expertise as unplugging an electric lamp and plugging it back in.

In this chapter, I give you the lowdown on caring for these devices so that you don't have to replace them before their time — and show you what to do when replacement day finally comes.

Keep Your Keyboard Clean

➡ **Never, *ever* get it wet.** Here's a rule that's more ignored than observed:

 Don't place a cup of coffee, a can of soda, or any other liquid anywhere near your keyboard — or your PC, for that matter. Spilled liquids are very likely to short out the electronics. Although you may be able to clean a keyboard that's been doused with soda, this is a problem that you don't need and can easily avoid.

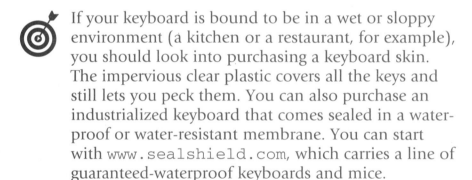 If your keyboard is bound to be in a wet or sloppy environment (a kitchen or a restaurant, for example), you should look into purchasing a keyboard skin. The impervious clear plastic covers all the keys and still lets you peck them. You can also purchase an industrialized keyboard that comes sealed in a water-proof or water-resistant membrane. You can start with www.sealshield.com, which carries a line of guaranteed-waterproof keyboards and mice.

➡ **Give it a good cleaning every few months.** To clean a keyboard, follow these steps:

1. Turn off the power to the PC, unplug the keyboard, and turn it over to shake out dust and dirt.

If you have a USB keyboard or mouse that attaches to your PC with a USB cable (see **Figure 13-1**), you can unplug it while the computer is turned on. If your mouse is old enough that it uses a PS/2 connector (see "Vet Your Mouse," later in this chapter), the safest way to proceed is to shut down the PC before removing the plug.

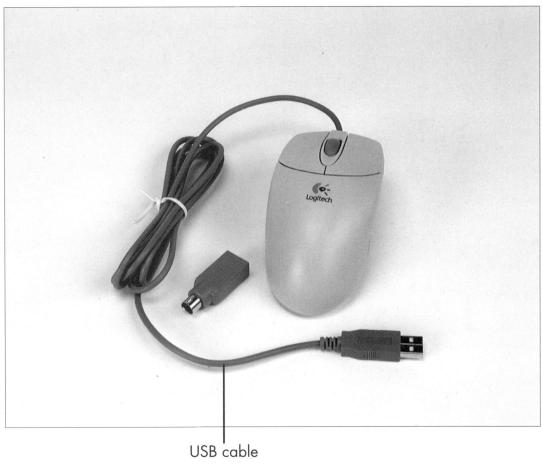

USB cable

Figure 13-1

2. For even better cleaning, use a can of compressed air (available at office-supply stores) to blow between individual keys, or use a vacuum cleaner's crevice-tool attachment to suck out dirt. This tool concentrates the power of the vacuum and can pull debris out from between and under the keys. Just use caution; this tool normally is made of hard plastic, so you don't want to be too aggressive with your cleaning.

 An excellent tool for cleaning the keyboard, screen, and other parts of the computer is a soft, unused paintbrush. I keep a couple of different sizes on or near my desk at all times. The soft bristles won't scratch hardware or screen surfaces, and they can reach between keys and into other cracks and crevices to remove dust and other undesirable debris (see **Figure 13-2**).

Use commercial air or a soft brush (even a clean paintbrush) to keep your keyboard shipshape.

Figure 13-2

3. Use a soft cloth dampened with a weak plastic cleaner or a small amount of isopropyl alcohol to polish the keys and the surrounding case. The most fastidious among you may want to use the same solution on a cotton swab to clean between the keys.

If it's absolutely necessary, you can remove individual keys with a special tool that's supplied with many keyboards; a technician's tweezers with hooked ends will also work. Work very carefully to avoid breaking the plastic keycaps or the somewhat delicate switches beneath them.

4. Let the keyboard dry for a half an hour or so.

You can use a hairdryer on low heat to speed the drying process. Just keep the air stream moving, and don't get the nozzle too close to sensitive plastic parts.

5. When the keyboard is nice and dry, reattach it to your computer.

You can plug in a USB keyboard while the computer is on. If your mouse is an older model with a PS/2 connector, reattach it before you turn on the power.

Diagnose a Troubled Keyboard

1. If the keyboard completely stops responding, check to see whether the device is connected properly at the computer end, and look for any cuts or crimps in the cable. Fix any loose connections and straighten any kinks; if the cable is cut, replace it.

2. If the connections and cable are fine, try rebooting the computer to see whether the keyboard comes back to life. With luck, you were experiencing a once-in-a-blue-moon system lockup.

 If the keyboard freezes more frequently than a blue moon, or if the intervals between freeze-ups begin to shorten, you may be seeing early symptoms of the impending failure of a major component, such as the motherboard or the power supply. Run a diagnostic program such as the one that ships with many computers, or take the computer to a repair shop for a good once-over.

3. Check the connection between the PC and the keyboard, as well as the status of the keyboard's device driver, as follows:

   a. Choose Start⇨Control Panel⇨Keyboard (XP) to open the Keyboard Properties dialog box. In Windows 7 and Vista this direct path is available from the icon view of the control panel.

   b. Click the Hardware tab. You should see the name or type of keyboard (listed in the Devices list), as well as the manufacturer and the means of communicating with the system.

   c. Check the Device Status entry to see whether the computer is communicating with the keyboard properly (see **Figure 13-3**).

   d. Click the Properties button to display another Properties dialog box; then click the Driver tab to examine the details of the driver and make any necessary changes or updates. (For details, see "Revive a Dead Mouse, Trackball, or Keyboard," later in this chapter.)

 You rarely have to make driver changes for a basic component such as a keyboard unless there's been some sort of electrical corruption of the device or the driver has been deleted or changed.

Click for error messages in
the Device Properties section.

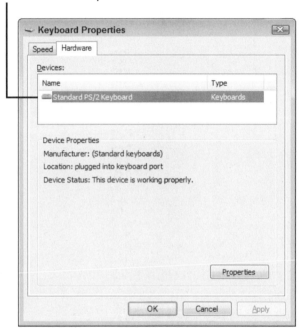

Figure 13-3

e. While you're in the neighborhood, you can close the second Properties dialog box and click the Speed tab of the Keyboard Properties dialog box (see **Figure 13-4**) to make a few adjustments in the response of the keyboard, such as the *repeat rate* (how quickly the keyboard produces a string of repeated characters when a key is held down).

These settings tell your keyboard how quickly to respond.

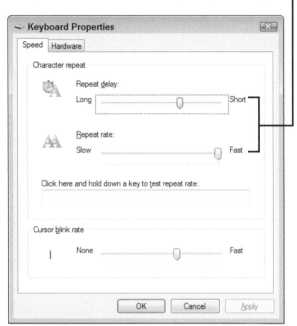

Figure 13-4

 You can also set the cursor's blink rate in this tab. This function really isn't related to the keyboard, but technicians had to put the control somewhere.

   f. Click OK to save your settings and close the dialog box.

4. Every few months (to be especially conscientious), run the keyboard test that's part of most diagnostic programs to test the electronic logic of the keyboard and the motherboard's keyboard controller. The test also forces you to run through all the keys on the board, including a few that you may not ordinarily use. Follow any instructions that the program gives you.

 If you're still having problems, turn to "Revive a Dead Mouse, Trackball, or Keyboard," later in this chapter.

Practice Good Mousekeeping

 Much of what I say about mice in this chapter also applies to trackballs and other pointing devices (see Chapter 1). Also, except where I indicate otherwise, these tips apply to both mechanical and optical mice.

➠ **Keep your desktop clean.** Your mouse travels miles and miles, sliding back and forth on your desktop. Along the way, it picks up dust, pollen, oils, cookie crumbs, and whatever else is floating around your office. Sooner or later, the going is going to get a bit sticky. To give your mouse a clear path, wipe off your desktop — and your mouse pad, if you use one — once a month or more often if you notice any kind of buildup on your mouse pad.

➠ **Give your mouse a bath.** If your mouse seems to have lost its way, the first thing to do is give it a good cleaning, like so:

• **Mechanical mouse:** Unplug the mouse from the computer, turn it over, and (on most mice) rotate the plastic or rubber ring to release the rubber roller ball (see **Figure 13-5**). Use a can of compressed air or the crevice-tool attachment of a vacuum cleaner to remove debris from the cavity. Then clean the ball (and rollers, if any) with mild soap and water or alcohol, using a lint-free cloth.

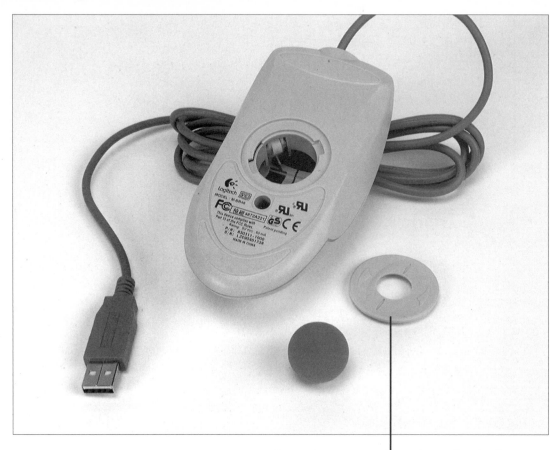

Twist this ring to free the roller ball.

Figure 13-5

- **Trackball:** A trackball is essentially an upside-down mechanical mouse with its roller ball built into a mouse body or even into a keyboard (see **Figure 13-6**). The ball rests loosely in a cavity, where sensors track horizontal and vertical movement. Instead of moving the hardware across the desk, you use your hand to spin the ball in place. You clean a trackball the same way that you clean a mechanical mouse. (See the manual for directions on how to remove the roller ball on your particular model.)

Spin this ball to move the mouse pointer.

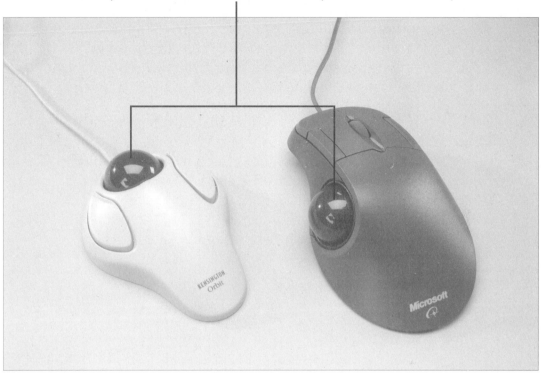

Figure 13-6

 You should clean a mechanical mouse or trackball every few months, whether or not you think it needs cleaning. Check the manual that came with your mouse for any specific instructions.

- **Optical mouse:** Cleaning an optical mouse is simple because it contains no moving parts. Use an alcohol cleaner or a small spray of window cleaner on a rag to remove any buildup from the sensor on its bottom.

Vet Your Mouse

1. If your mouse or other pointing device is acting peculiar, first make sure that it's connected to the computer properly. Fix any loose connections, and adjust or replace any twisted or damaged cable.

2. If the connection is fine, choose Start⇨Control Panel⇨ Mouse (in Classic View in Vista and Windows 7) to open the Mouse Properties dialog box. Click the Hardware tab and then click Properties (see **Figure 13-7**) to see whether Windows is reporting a failure of a USB port (or a PS/2 serial port, if you have an older mouse that uses that type of port, such as the one shown in **Figure 13-8**).

Check location and device status.

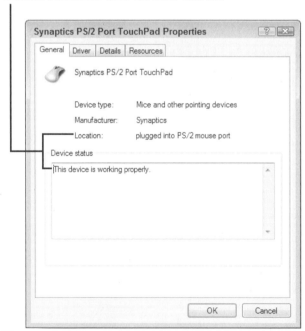

Figure 13-7

PS/2 serial port connection for older mouse

Figure 13-8

3. If you see no report of a problem with a port, click the
Driver tab of this dialog box to check for conflicts or
problems with device drivers (see "Revive a Dead Mouse,
Trackball, or Keyboard," later in this chapter).

 You should also consult the manufacturer's Web site
to see whether updated or corrected device drivers
have been released for your mouse.

4. To adjust the ways in which your mouse responds, click the other tabs of the Mouse Properties dialog box (such as the Buttons tab, shown in **Figure 13-9**), and make any changes you want. Each manufacturer offers different types of adjustments for its mouse device, so the tabs in your dialog box may differ from those in the figure.

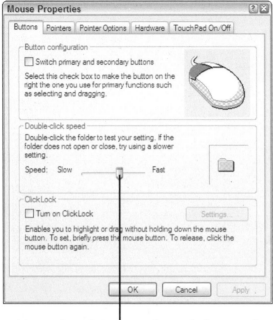

Move this slider to adjust click speed
Figure 13-9

5. Click OK to save your changes and close the dialog box.

6. If your mouse or trackball came with a control program for setting up special features, the same program usually offers basic test software. Run this software to see how your mouse is performing, and follow any onscreen instructions.

 If you're still having problems, read on; the next section of this chapter may help.

Revive a Dead Mouse, Trackball, or Keyboard

1. If your mouse, trackball, or keyboard isn't functioning at all, restart the computer in safe mode (see Chapter 17).

Restarting in safe mode is also the thing to do if you somehow disabled the keyboard or pointing device and can't use either to get where you need to go to set matters right.

2. Working in safe mode, you should be able to repair or rest the device's driver in Device Manager (see Chapter 18).

3. If the hardware itself has failed — which eventually will be the case with mechanical devices like these — the solution is to unplug the old and plug in the new, as I describe in the next section.

If you've decided that your keyboard or mouse is beyond repair, you can try a radical approach: Put it in the dishwasher. Although no hardware manufacturer officially sanctions this sort of repair, people do it, and I've done it myself. Use a gentle cycle, cool dry, with little or no soap, and let the device dry out for a week or so before you plug it in again. You have nothing to lose, and this method *does* work sometimes.

Replace a Dead Mouse, Trackball, or Keyboard

1. Remove the deceased device from your computer.

- **USB devices:** You can leave the computer on while you disconnect (see **Figure 13-10**).

- **PS/2 devices:** Turn the computer off before you disconnect.

You can attach and detach a USB keyboard while your PC is running.

Figure 13-10

2. Plug in the replacement keyboard or pointing device.

3. If you turned the computer off in Step 1, turn it back on.

4. Follow all instructions from the maker of the replacement device to install the new device's driver or utility
program.

I recommend that you always have a replacement
mouse or trackball and keyboard on hand. Like hard
drives and other mechanical elements of a PC, these
devices are bound to fail sooner or later. Keeping
replacements in your supply closet (they won't go
stale) can save you time and aggravation.

Part IV
Resetting the Operating System

The 5th Wave   By Rich Tennant

"Oddly enough, it came with a PCI bus slot."

Repairing, Refreshing, and Reinstalling Windows

W hen you buy a new PC from a retailer or directly from a manufacturer, it ordinarily comes with Windows already installed. It's almost always better — both financially and technically — to get Windows this way. The maker of the computer should have installed all the necessary drivers and made any necessary tweaks in settings to match the particular combination of hardware in the box.

In four situations, however, you may need to install or reinstall Windows yourself:

➠ Adding a new hard disk drive to replace the original boot drive (see Chapter 11)

➠ Repairing an existing installation of Windows

➠ Reinstalling the existing operating system to fix otherwise-irreparable damage

➠ Upgrading Windows from one version to another

In this chapter, I show you how to repair and replace Windows on your PC.

 Be sure to keep the alphanumeric product key that came with your Windows installation disc. You can't install Windows properly without this key.

Repair a Windows XP Installation

1. Choose Start⇨Turn Off Computer⇨Restart to restart your computer, and watch the screen carefully. You should see a message to press a function key (F2 probably) or another key combination to enter the BIOS (Basic Input Output System) screen. See the manufacturer's documentation for more information on your particular computer.

2. Press the designated key or key combination. You have only a few seconds to press this key to interrupt the startup process and enter the BIOS screen.

3. Look for an option called First Boot Device, Boot Sequence, or something similar. (You may have to select Advanced Options or another submenu to find it.) Press the arrow keys on your keyboard to select this field; then press Enter.

4. In the resulting screen, select CDROM/DVD.

5. Press the Esc key until you return to the main BIOS screen.

6. Follow the onscreen instructions to save your new settings and exit BIOS setup. Your computer will restart from the CD/DVD drive.

7. Insert your Windows XP Setup CD into the drive.

 Some computer manufacturers tried to save a few pennies by not providing a copy of the Windows disc with the systems they ship. If you didn't receive a Windows disc with your computer, the maker may have placed a recovery utility in a separate partition on the computer's original hard drive. Visit the manufacturer's Web site for advice on how to access that hidden partition during startup.

 The problem with this sort of hidden partition is that it doesn't allow you to install Windows on a replacement hard disk drive. You'll have to purchase physical Windows discs from the computer maker or from a computer store.

8. Restart your computer. A startup screen like the one shown in **Figure 14-1** appears. (Depending on the Windows or setup discs you have for your computer, you may see a slightly different menu.)

 You may see an interim message that asks you to confirm that you want to start from the CD/DVD drive. Follow the onscreen instructions (which usually are to press any key).

9. Choose Install Windows XP.

10. In the next screen, if you're asked whether you want to install Windows XP now, select that option. (Don't choose the option to use the Recovery Console.)

11. In the next screen, press F8 to accept the Windows XP licensing agreement.

Choose Install Windows XP.

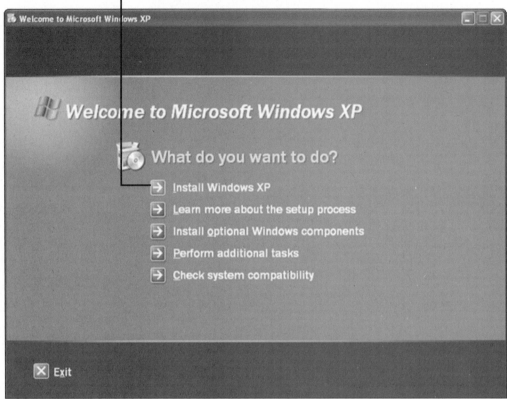

Figure 14-1

12. If you have multiple operating systems or multiple versions of Windows installed on your computer, the next screen displays a list of those operating systems. Choose the one you want to repair or reinstall. **Figure 14-2** shows this screen for a PC with only one version of Windows installed, which is the normal configuration.

13. Press the R key on your keyboard to repair the operating system.

14. Follow the onscreen instructions.

Select the operating system you want to reinstall or repair.

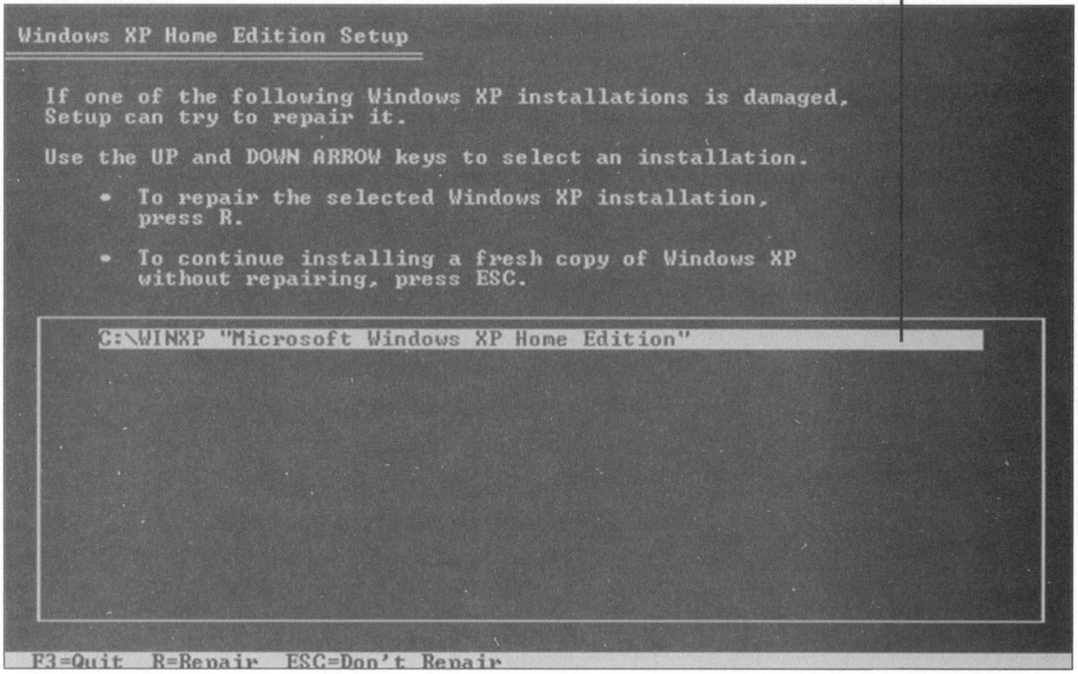

```
Windows XP Home Edition Setup

If one of the following Windows XP installations is damaged,
Setup can try to repair it.

Use the UP and DOWN ARROW keys to select an installation.

    •  To repair the selected Windows XP installation,
       press R.

    •  To continue installing a fresh copy of Windows XP
       without repairing, press ESC.

    C:\WINXP "Microsoft Windows XP Home Edition"




F3=Quit   R=Repair   ESC=Don't Repair
```

Figure 14-2

Repair a Vista or Windows 7 Installation

1. Choose Start⟹Turn Off Computer⟹Restart to restart your
computer, and watch the screen carefully. You should see
a message to press a function key (F2 probably) or
another key combination to enter the BIOS (Basic Input
Output System) screen. See the manufacturer's documentation for more information on your particular computer.

2. Press the designated key or key combination. You have
only a few seconds to press this key to interrupt the
startup process and enter the BIOS screen.

3. Look for an option called First Boot Device, Boot Sequence, or something similar. (You may have to select Advanced Options or another submenu to find it.) Press the arrow keys on your keyboard to select this field; then press Enter.

4. In the resulting screen, select CDROM/DVD.

5. Press the Esc key until you return to the main BIOS screen.

6. Follow the onscreen instructions to save your new settings and exit BIOS setup. Your computer will restart from the CD/DVD drive.

7. Insert the Windows Vista or Windows 7 installation CD into the drive.

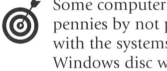 Some computer manufacturers tried to save a few pennies by not providing a copy of the Windows disc with the systems they ship. If you didn't receive a Windows disc with your computer, the maker may have placed a recovery utility in a separate partition on the computer's original hard drive. Read the instruction manual for advice on how to access that hidden partition during startup.

 The problem with this sort of hidden partition is that it doesn't allow you to install Windows on a replacement hard disk drive. You'll have to purchase physical Windows discs from the computer maker or from a computer store.

8. Restart your computer.

9. If you're prompted to do so, press any key to start the Windows installation from the CD/DVD drive.

10. In the resulting screen, select language settings, and click Next.

11. In the next screen, click Repair Your Computer.

12. In the next screen, select the operating system or version of Windows that you want to repair, and click Next.

> If the maker of your computer preinstalled the recovery software on your hard drive, check the Web site for directions on how to proceed. You may be asked to press one of the function keys as the system restarts to go to a hidden partition.

13. In the System Recovery Options window, select Startup Repair (see **Figure 14-3**). The utility scans your installation of Windows to determine which files need to be repaired or replaced.

14. Follow any onscreen instructions.

Select Startup Repair to begin the process.

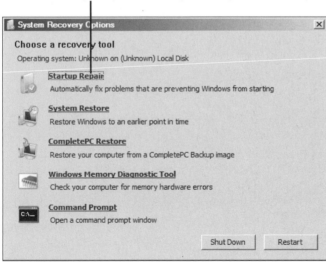

Figure 14-3

If you're asked whether you want to replace a current version of a file with an older version, click No. If the installation process finds a newer version of a file on your computer, it means that you've upgraded the file from an online source; you should keep the newer file.

15. Wait to see what the utility reports:

- **Successful repair:** If the problem with your Windows installation is relatively minor, Startup Repair may be able to bring it back to health without erasing your software and personal files.

- **Failure to repair:** If Startup Repair can't cure your PC's illness, it displays a report that provides some details on the problem. Make full notes, and discuss the issue with the manufacturer's support department or a repair technician.

 Startup Repair can't correct hardware failures, such as a failing hard disk drive that corrupts files. (See Chapter 11 for more info on hard drives.) Also, it can't remove all the tendrils of a virus. A capable security software program should scrub away all traces of viruses and other forms of malware (see Chapter 6).

Refresh Windows

Another option is reinstalling Windows over the existing version — a process called *refreshing*. Refreshing may fix a few problems that repairing doesn't, but it can't fix viruses or conflicts between versions of system files. The process I describe in this section applies to all current versions of Windows, though the precise screens you see will be a little different in each Windows version. To do a refresh, follow these steps:

1. Start your computer from the CD/DVD drive, as described in Steps 1–6 of the preceding two sections.

2. Insert your Windows installation disc into the drive.

3. Restart your computer. You see a screen similar to the one shown in **Figure** 14-4.

4. Select the Install Now option.

Don't choose an option to change partitions or reformat the drive. Either option would erase all your software and personal data.

5. Follow the onscreen instructions.

Choose Install Now.

Figure 14-4

Know When to Reinstall Windows

If repair attempts fail (see "Repair a Windows XP Installation" or "Repair a Vista or Windows 7 Installation," earlier in this chapter), and if refreshing doesn't have the desired effect (see "Refresh Windows," earlier in this chapter), reinstalling Windows should fix almost any problem. Reinstallation works best if:

➠ The manufacturer supplied a restore disk with the computer. That disk returns a PC to its original factory-delivered state. If you don't have a restore disk, you have to perform an ordinary installation from the original Windows discs.

You may be able to fix things with System Restore (see **Figure 14-5**). This process returns your system to an earlier state — before you installed updates or third-party software — but doesn't affect your data files.

➠ Your computer is able to start, and you can get to the operating system.

➠ You can make backup copies of all your personal data. The easiest way to do this is to plug in an external hard disk drive (see Chapter 11) and copy the files from your computer to the external drive. You can also make backups on a DVD (about 4.7GB of data) or on a CD (about 700MB of data) if your computer is capable of burning discs and if the CD/DVD drive is functioning.

The bad news? A complete reinstallation wipes the hard drive clean, removing all software and all your personal files. Also, reinstalling Windows won't fix any problems with misbehaving hardware or incompatible devices that you added on your own.

(You may be able to obtain assistance from the makers of those pieces of hardware, including updated device drivers and other adaptations that make the products work better with Windows.)

Select Recommended Restore, and click Next.

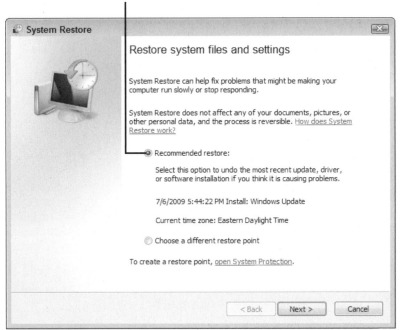

Figure 14-5

Reinstall Windows

1. Make copies of all the personal files on your computer: word processing, spreadsheet, database, photos, videos, music, and so on. You don't need to make backup copies of your software programs; you'll need to reinstall those programs anyway when Windows is back in place.

2. Start your computer from the CD/DVD drive, as described in Steps 1–6 of "Repair a Windows XP Installation" or "Repair a Vista or Windows 7 Installation" earlier in this chapter.

3. Insert your Windows installation CD into the drive.

4. Restart your computer.

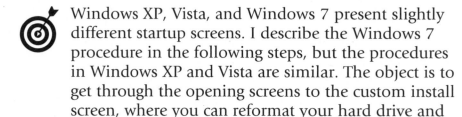 Windows XP, Vista, and Windows 7 present slightly different startup screens. I describe the Windows 7 procedure in the following steps, but the procedures in Windows XP and Vista are similar. The object is to get through the opening screens to the custom install screen, where you can reformat your hard drive and begin a clean installation.

5. In the startup screen, select the Install Now option.

6. In the next screen, select I Accept the License Terms, and click the Next button.

7. When you're asked what kind of installation you want to do, select Custom (Advanced).

8. If you're given a choice of partitions, select the one in which you want to install Windows. In most cases, you have only one or two choices: maybe a small partition (200MB or so) and a large one (30GB–100GB or larger). Select the larger partition for your Windows installation.

9. In the next screen, click Advanced to expand the options at the bottom of the screen, and choose the option to reformat your drive.

10. Follow the onscreen instructions to reformat your drive and install Windows.

11. When you're prompted to do so, enter the Windows product key (see the example in **Figure 14-6**). This key — a set of 25 letters and numbers — may be on the Windows CD/DVD case or on a separate sheet of paper that came with the software. Some manufacturers also place a copy of the key on a sticker affixed to the computer case.

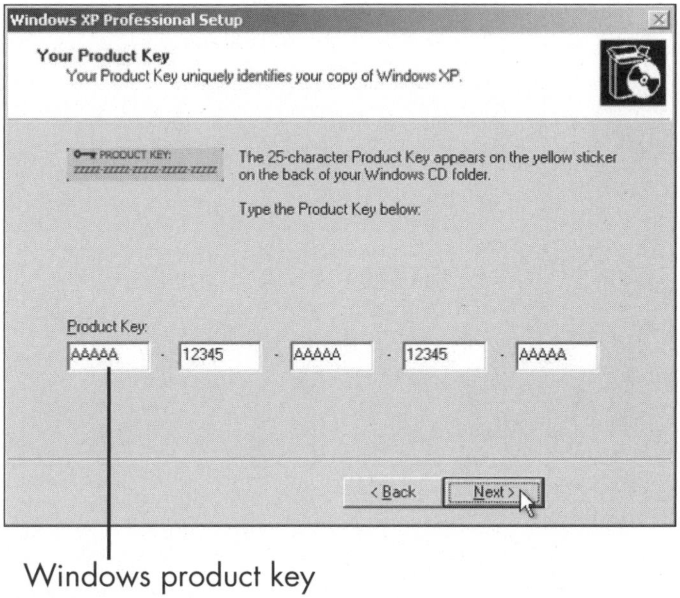

Windows product key

Figure 14-6

12. Follow the onscreen instructions to complete the job.

Checking and Changing System Configuration

You and I are sentient beings. We can perceive our world. PCs, however, know *nothing*. All they can do is move around numbers that humans have placed in their nonliving memory.

But every computer has a feature that gives it a personality of sorts, as well as information about its parts and capabilities. This feature falls under the general category of system configuration or system setup.

Part of this setup or configuration information is stored in a special part of the computer's memory where it won't get lost when the power is turned off (the BIOS). Part of it is stored on the system's hard drive. This foundational memory tells the computer about its world — what disk drives are attached, what other kinds of memory it has, and other details involving all the hardware that makes up the machine.

This information is stored when the computer is built. Sometimes, it's useful to look at this data to reconfigure the PC or help identify problems.

In this chapter, I show you how to use the System Configuration tool to search for the sources of problems caused by corrupted, missing, or misassigned programs and elements of Windows.

 Very technical elements of system configuration, such as setting BIOS (Basic Input and Output System) and CMOS (Complimentary Metal Oxide Silicon, a type of solid-state memory), are beyond the scope of this book. You may want to leave this type of configuration to an expert.

View and Document System Setup Screens

 Here's an example of the process for viewing system setup information on a Dell Dimension PC. Your PC may have a slightly different procedure.

1. Turn on or restart the computer, and watch the monitor closely. When you see the blue Dell logo, the F2 prompt should appear soon afterward (see **Figure 15-1**). This prompt indicates that the BIOS has *initialized* the keyboard — prepared it for first use.

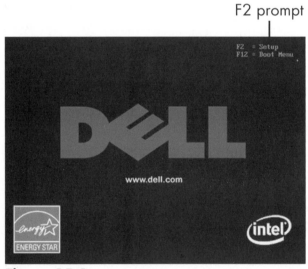

Figure 15-1

2. Immediately press the F2 key on your keyboard. After a short pause, a system-setup screen should appear. Your PC may display slightly different information from the screen shown in **Figure 15-2**.

Navigation pane

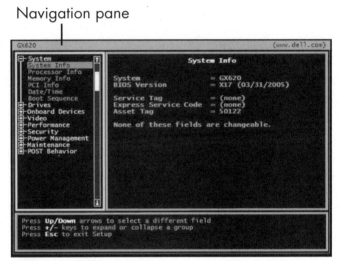

Figure 15-2

 If you press F2 too late, your PC will proceed to load Windows. Don't turn it off; wait for Windows to load, restart your computer, and try again.

3. Select options in the navigation pane by using the arrow keys on your keyboard to scroll up and down through the navigation pane. (You need to use the arrow keys because your mouse or other pointing device probably won't be working this early in the startup process.) As you select each option, the screen displays details on current and available settings.

 Depending on the design of your PC's setup screen, pressing the Enter key or arrow keys expands or collapses a list of available options. The onscreen display should tell you how to navigate the list.

4. Write down all the settings you see in each screen.

 Some people use a digital camera to take close-up images of setup screens. If you go this route, make sure that you can read all the information in the images.

5. Consult the instruction manual or online support pages for your computer model to find a list of your computer's standard (default) settings, and identify the process for restoring all the settings to their original default condition. You may not want or need to use this emergency parachute, but someday, it may be the way to get out of an otherwise-unresolvable technical bind.

 Store all the information you've gathered — including handwritten notes or digital photographs — with the rest of your computer documentation so that it's available if you need it later to solve a configuration problem.

6. Press the Esc key one or more times until you see a prompt that asks whether you want to exit this utility or save the data and exit. You should not have changed anything during this inspection tour, so select the exit option. Your system should resume the normal startup process and return you to Windows.

View System Configuration in Windows XP

1. Choose Start⇨Run to open the Run dialog box.

2. Type **msconfig** in the Open text box, and click OK. The System Configuration Utility dialog box appears (see **Figure 15-3**), displaying seven tabs:

Tabs

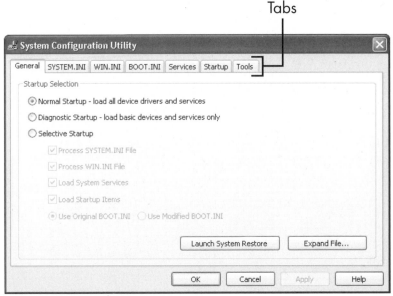

Figure 15-3

- General

- SYSTEM.INI

- WIN.INI

- BOOT.INI

- Services

- Startup

- Tools

Each of these tabs contains settings for various elements of your PC. In the following steps, I cover the ones that you may want to investigate.

 It's best to stay away from all the .INI tabs. You can't change much on those tabs to help solve problems, and changing some settings could really mess things up.

3. Click the Services tab, which displays a long list of the current software services running in Windows. Most of these services won't mean a whole lot to you, but it's interesting and surprising to see what's loaded on your computer. If you're using this utility to solve a problem, see "Select Diagnostic Startup," later in this chapter.

4. Click the Startup tab, which lists the programs that launch every time you start your machine. You'll recognize some applications that you use regularly, such as Microsoft Office or your antivirus program. The ones you don't recognize are launchers or helpers for other hardware and software that help improve performance or are required for some operations.

5. Click the Tools tab, which lists the software tools you can use to inspect or troubleshoot your system. (Interestingly, Microsoft's help-desk technicians may use the same tools to help you uncover and repair a problem with your computer.)

 You can experiment with these tools, but use caution. Tools such as Registry Editor can cause some serious system ills if they're used incorrectly.

6. When you're ready to get on with other computer tasks, click the OK button to close the System Configuration Utility dialog box.

Select Diagnostic Startup in Windows XP

 It certainly is interesting to poke around inside the System Configuration Utility (see the preceding section), but you also can use it as a serious diagnostic tool.

1. Choose Start⇨Run to open the Run dialog box, type **msconfig** in the Open text box, and click OK to open the System Configuration Utility dialog box.

2. On the General tab, select Diagnostic Startup, and click OK. The utility takes a few seconds to disable all but the most essential startup programs and services.

3. When the Restart/Exit prompt appears, click Restart.

4. When the diagnostics notification appears, click OK. Windows displays the System Configuration Utility dialog box again.

5. Click the Startup tab, scan the list for a program that's a likely troublemaker, and check its check box.

   You recognize a troublemaker through a process of elimination and good guessing. Analyze the problem that you're experiencing, and try to find an application that may have something to do with it. I suggest starting with anything that isn't a Microsoft product and, therefore, may be incompatible with Windows.

6. Click OK to restart your computer in Selective Startup mode.

7. If the problem recurs, proceed to Step 8. If the problem doesn't occur, repeat the steps until you locate the offending application.

8. Reinstall the problem program or contact the software manufacturer for help.

9. Follow the steps in the next section to return your system to normal startup.

Return to Normal Startup in Windows XP

1. Choose Start⇨Run to open the Run dialog box.

2. Type **msconfig** in the Open text box, and click OK. The System Configuration Utility dialog box opens.

3. On the General tab, select Normal Startup, and click OK. Your computer restarts with all its programs enabled.

View System Configuration in Vista and Windows 7

1. Click the Start button and then click inside the Search Programs and Files field (Start Search in Vista) at the bottom of the screen. The msconfig program appears at the top of the search box.

2. Click msconfig to display the System Configuration dialog box. Vista displays a UserAccount Control notice.

3. Investigate the Services, Startup, and Tools tabs, which are essentially the same as those in the System Configuration Utility dialog box in Windows XP (see "View System Configuration in Windows XP," earlier in this chapter).

Missing from the System Configuration dialog box, however, are the .INI tabs from Windows XP — which is probably a good thing, because you shouldn't change those settings anyway.

4. Click the Boot tab to display the dialog box shown in **Figure 15-4**.

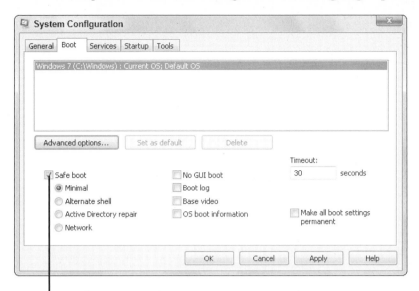

Select Safe Boot and then experiment with
different settings for troubleshooting.
Figure 15-4

5. Click the General tab, choose Diagnostic Startup, and
click OK to test your system with minimal applications
loaded (see "Select Diagnostic Startup in Windows XP,"
earlier in this chapter).

6. When your testing is complete, select Normal Startup on
the General tab, and click OK to return to normal startup
mode. Your computer restarts with all its applications
enabled.

Restoring Your Computer's Settings

*I*f your PC ran fine yesterday (or just a few minutes ago), but all of a sudden it won't load Windows, ask yourself this essential question: What has changed since the last time this computer performed properly? Here are a few possible answers:

⟹ You installed new software.

⟹ You uninstalled or deleted software.

⟹ Microsoft or another software company delivered a major update to your computer.

⟹ You installed new or updated device drivers.

⟹ You recently changed the settings or configuration of Windows.

⟹ You deleted or changed one of the system files of Windows or another program.

⟹ The lights just dimmed or the power went out, perhaps because of an electrical storm.

Any of these events could result in unexpected, unwanted changes in critical files on your computer. Fortunately, you may be able to turn back the clock to resolve problems. I show you how in this chapter.

 If you recently installed new hardware inside your PC, or if an existing piece of hardware has failed, you should start by troubleshooting the equipment, not the software.

Undo Something You Just Did

1. Start Windows in safe mode. This mode loads only the most basic functionality for things like the keyboard and mouse, and displays a different screen from what you're used to seeing. **Figure 16-1** provides additional information. For details, see Chapter 17.

2. When you have Windows running in this limited mode, undo the changes you just made.

3. Restart the computer.

Uninstall a Problematic Program

1. Follow the appropriate step for your version of Windows:

- **Windows XP:** Choose Start⇨Control Panel to open the Control Panel window; then double-click the Add or Remove Programs icon to open the Add or Remove Programs window.

- **Vista and Windows 7:** Choose Start⇨Control Panel to open the Control Panel window. Then (in Classic View) select Programs and Features or (in

Category View) select Uninstall a Program in the
Programs category. Either action opens the
Uninstall or Change a Program window.

Use Windows Help at any time to learn more about Windows topics.

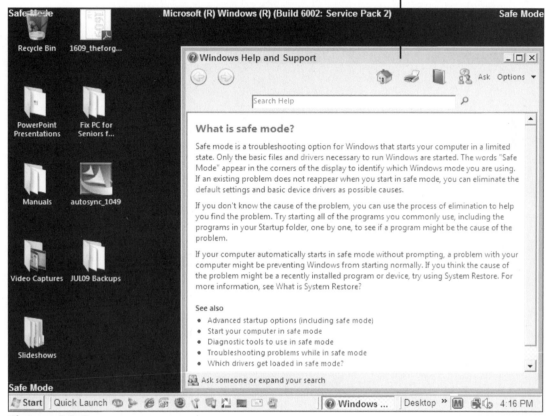

Figure 16-1

2. Select the program that you want to remove.

If you're not certain that this program is causing the
problem, you could try the repair option in Windows
7 first. If that doesn't work, proceed with the
uninstallation.

3. Click the button titled something like Change/Remove, Uninstall/Change, or Uninstall. The name of this button or option may differ from program to program. Some programs provide a Change button that opens a separate utility in which you can modify or remove the program; others offer a Remove button that does just that. Still other programs have a single button called Change/Remove that offers a more complex set of options. **Figure 16-2** shows one program's response after the Uninstall/Change button is clicked.

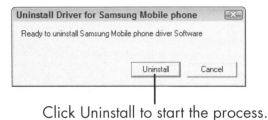

Click Uninstall to start the process.

Figure 16-2

4. Follow the onscreen instructions to remove the program. When the selected program is removed, you should see a confirmation dialog box like the one shown in **Figure 16-3**.

Click OK to close the confirmation dialog box.

Figure 16-3

 Also see Chapter 4 for more information on trouble-shooting and uninstalling misbehaving software.

Choose the Right Utility to Solve Your Problem

When all else fails, the next step is restoring earlier settings on your computer. Windows has two built-in utilities for this purpose: System Restore and Last Known Good Configuration. I cover both later in this chapter. To decide which to use, consider the primary differences:

→ System Restore can be used only on a PC that can start in Windows in either normal or safe mode (see Chapter 17).

→ Last Known Good Configuration can be invoked during the startup process and *may* be able to bring to life a PC that otherwise can't load Windows.

→ You can undo changes made with System Restore by repeating the process, going back to the settings that were in effect before the restore, or trying a different date in the hope of getting a different result.

→ Changes made through Last Known Good Configuration are permanent and cannot be undone.

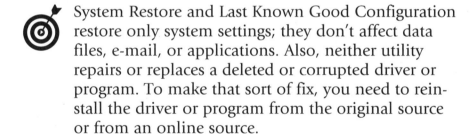 System Restore and Last Known Good Configuration restore only system settings; they don't affect data files, e-mail, or applications. Also, neither utility repairs or replaces a deleted or corrupted driver or program. To make that sort of fix, you need to reinstall the driver or program from the original source or from an online source.

Reset Your PC with System Restore

System Restore, featured in all current version of Windows, is a computer version of a time warp, allowing you to go back from the future to a specific *restore point* — a group of settings that were in effect last night, last week, or at some other time. By default, it creates restore points automatically every day, but you can also create them at any time (see the "Create a Restore Point Manually" section for your version of Windows, later in this chapter). System Restore is most likely to work if you use it immediately after you notice problems.

 You can use System Restore to reset your computer only if you've previously turned this feature on. There's really no reason not to use it, because it's enabled as part of a standard Windows installation.

1. Save any open files on your computer, and close all programs.

2. Make sure that you have current backups of essential data files.

3. Launch System Restore in any of the following ways:

- **Windows XP, Vista, and Windows 7:** Choose Start⇨All Programs⇨Accessories⇨System Tools⇨ System Restore.

- **Vista only:** Click the Start button, type **system restore** in the Search box, and then click the utility's name in the search results.

- **Windows 7 only:** Click the Start button, type **system restore** in the Search box, and then click Restore Your Computer to an Earlier Time.

The resulting window asks whether you want to create a restore point (set one manually) or choose a previously recorded restore point. **Figure 16-4** shows this window in Windows XP; the Vista and Windows 7 windows are slightly different.

Choose this option in Windows XP.

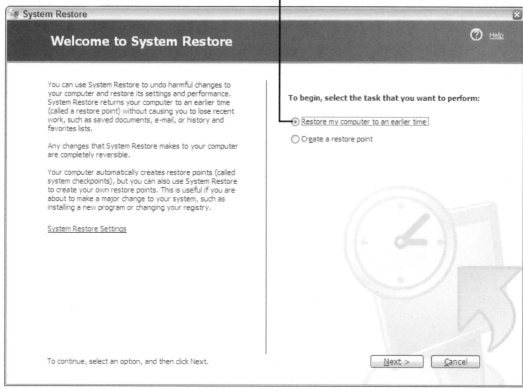

Figure 16-4

4. Follow the appropriate step for your version of Windows:

- **Windows XP:** Select Restore My Computer to an Earlier Time, and click the Next button.

- **Vista:** Select Recommended Restore or Choose a Different Restore Point (see **Figure 16-5**), and click the Next button.

- **Windows 7:** Select Open System Restore, and click the Next button.

Choose one of these options in Vista.

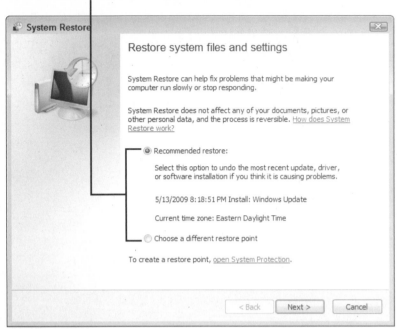

Figure 16-5

5. In the next window, select a restore point (preferably one just before the day and time when you began experiencing problems). **Figure 16-6** shows this window in Windows XP; **Figure 16-7** shows the Vista version of the window; and **Figure 16-8** shows the Windows 7 version.

Select a date in this calendar in Windows XP.

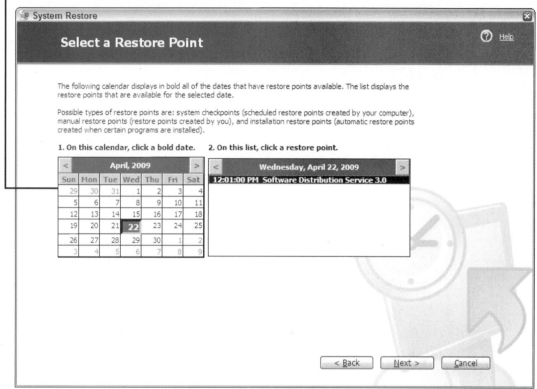

Figure 16-6

Choose a restore point in Vista.

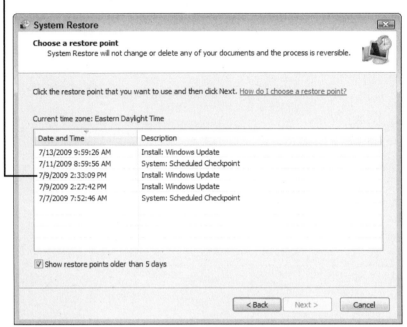

Figure 16-7

Choose a restore point in Windows 7.

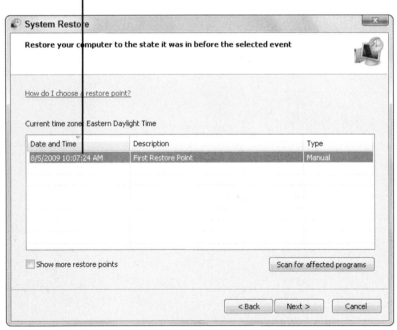

Figure 16-8

Don't go too far back in time. Going farther back than necessary could disable good updates and changes that you made before the problem started. Try using restore points created just before problems started. If the first restore doesn't work, go farther back.

6. Click the Next button. The computer chugs along for a few moments, preparing the information it needs, and then restarts.

7. When your PC restarts, follow the appropriate step:

- **Successful restoration:** If the restoration is successful, you see a screen like the one shown in **Figure 16-9** when Windows loads. Click the Finish button to close System Restore.

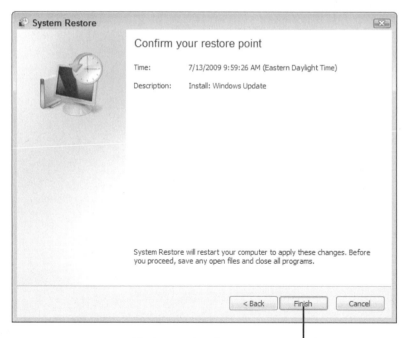

Click Finish after a successful restoration

Figure 16-9

- **Failed restoration:** If the restoration fails, your computer restarts in the same condition it was in before you attempted to fix it. Repeat Steps 3–6 with a different restore point.

 To undo restoration changes, open System Restore; select the Undo System Restore radio button (see **Figure 16-10**); and click Next. You won't see the option to undo a system restore until you've done a system restore.

Choose Undo System Restore, and click Next.

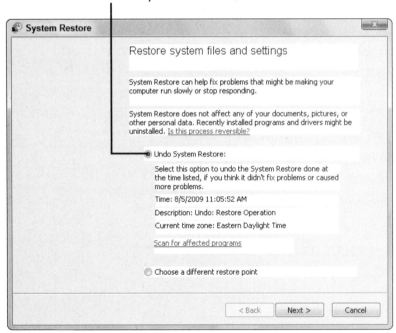

Figure 16-10

 As a safeguard against future problems, I recommend that you create a restore point manually before you add a program or change a major setting. The following sections show you how.

Create a Restore Point Manually in Windows XP

1. Choose Start⇨All Programs⇨Accessories⇨System Tools⇨ System Restore. The Welcome to System Restore window opens (refer to Figure 16-4 earlier in this chapter).

2. Select the Create a Restore Point radio button, and click the Next button.

3. Follow the onscreen instructions.

Create a Restore Point Manually in Vista

1. Choose Start⇨All Programs⇨Accessories⇨System Tools⇨System Restore.

or

Click the Start button, type **system restore** in the Search box, and then click the utility's name in the search results. (Vista shows a User Account Control window.)

Whichever method you use, the System Restore window opens.

2. Click the Open System Protection link, and click Create in the System Properties window.

3. Follow the onscreen instructions.

Create a Restore Point Manually in Windows 7

1. Choose Start⇨Control Panel⇨System, and click Change Settings to open the System Properties dialog box.

2. On the System Protection tab, click the Create button
(see **Figure 16-11**).

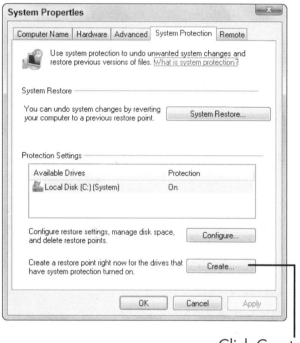

Click Create.

Figure 16-11

Windows automatically adds the date and time, and you
can include a short note, such as *Before changing mouse
device driver*.

Revert to the Last Known Good Configuration

Last Known Good Configuration restores the settings that were in
effect the last time the computer started successfully. It's not quite the
same as System Restore (see "Reset Your PC with System Restore," earlier in this chapter), which you can invoke days or weeks later to reset
a computer to an earlier configuration.

This tool should be your first line of defense if you just installed a new piece of hardware or software and find that the computer won't restart properly.

1. Remove any discs from the CD and/or DVD drives that may be part of your system.

2. Restart your computer.

3. As the computer comes to life — and before the Windows logo appears — repeatedly press and release the F8 function key. In a moment, the somewhat-scary Last Known Good Configuration screen should appear (see **Figure 16-12**).

 If the Windows logo appears instead, you've missed your moment. Wait until Windows has loaded fully; then shut down and restart to try again.

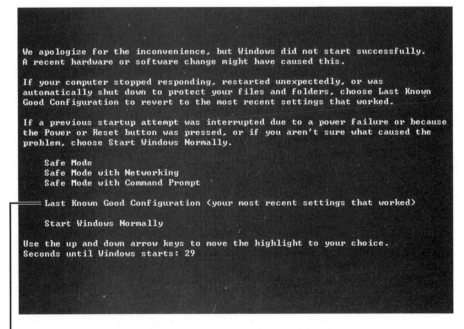

Press the arrow keys in your keyboard to select this option.

Figure 16-12

4. At this stage of the process, your mouse won't work, so use the arrow keys to highlight Last Known Good Configuration; then press the Enter key.

5. If you have more than one version of Windows installed on your PC, you see options for each version; choose the version that you want to restart. After you make your selection, your PC restarts in the selected version of Windows.

6. Inspect Windows applications, and test whatever caused you to choose this option in the first place to see whether you corrected the problem.

Working in Safe Mode

Safe mode is like putting your car up on a lift at the garage. When you run a computer in this mode, you can start it, test most of its systems, and change certain settings, but you're not going to get much use out of it until you bring it back down to Earth . . . and normal operations.

Safe mode is an excellent way to determine the source of problems:

⟶ If you can start your PC in safe mode, its basic hardware probably isn't the cause of your problem. Instead, the problem may involve settings or configurations that you recently made (see Chapter 4 and the chapters in Part IV), new devices that you recently added (see Part III), an electrical problem (see Chapter 9), or malware (see Chapter 6).

⟶ If you can't start your PC in safe mode, you have a problem with basic hardware (see Part III) or the basic elements of Windows (see Part IV).

⟶ If your PC starts in safe mode all by itself, some component is preventing normal startup. For help, see the "Test Components and Settings in Safe Mode" section of this chapter.

In this chapter, I show you how to use safe mode to diagnose — and often fix — your computer's problems.

Start Your Computer in Safe Mode

1. Remove any discs from the CD/DVD drive, if your PC has one.

2. Shut down your computer in one of the following ways:

- If you can see enough of the screen to follow the standard Windows shutdown procedure, do that.

- If you can't do a normal shutdown, press the Ctrl+Alt+Del key combination and then release the keys. (Whether you can see it or not, you're displaying Windows Task Manager.) Next, press and release the Alt key; press the U key to select the Shut Down menu; and press the U key to turn off the computer. (This works in XP, but not in Vista or Windows 7.)

3. Wait a few moments to allow the computer to shut off fully; then restart. The computer begins processing its self-test, and you should be able to see messages on the screen, including advice on alternative ways to start the computer. When the self-test is complete, the computer pauses briefly before it begins to load Windows.

4. During this pause, repeatedly press and release the F8 function key on the keyboard. Keep doing so until the Windows Advanced Options Menu screen appears (see **Figure 17-1**).

Select the Safe Mode option.

```
Windows Advanced Options Menu
Please select an option:

    Safe Mode
    Safe Mode with Networking
    Safe Mode with Command Prompt

    Enable Boot Logging
    Enable VGA Mode
    Last Known Good Configuration (your most recent settings that worked)
    Directory Services Restore Mode (Windows domain controllers only)
    Debugging Mode

    Start Windows Normally
    Reboot
    Return to OS Choices Menu

Use the up and down arrow keys to move the highlight to your choice.
```

Figure 17-1

 If you begin tapping the F8 key too soon, you'll see a "keyboard error" message; restart the computer and try again. If you begin tapping too late, the computer will go on to load Windows, and you have to repeat the shutdown/startup process.

5. If you have more than one version of Windows installed on your computer, use the arrow keys to select the version you want to start in safe mode, and then press F8; otherwise, go on to Step 6.

6. Press the arrow keys on the keyboard to highlight the Safe Mode option, and press Enter. The computer starts loading Windows in safe mode.

When Windows is fully loaded in safe mode, you see a basic screen like the one shown in **Figure 17-2** — probably using a smaller number of colors than you're used to seeing, as well as lower resolution, and displaying the words

Safe Mode in the corners. (To make the display more legible, see "Make the Monitor Easier to Read in Safe Mode," later in this chapter.)

Note the "Safe Mode" flags in the screen corners.

Figure 17-2

 The Safe Mode option starts Windows in a basic, limited mode. As you operate in this mode, you'll discover things that you can't do. You can select a more advanced option to perform additional troubleshooting, as I discuss in "Choose Advanced Safe Mode Options," later in this chapter.

Make the Monitor Easier to Read in Safe Mode

By default, safe mode uses a screen resolution of 800 x 600 pixels, but you can increase resolution to fit more on the screen and to produce a clearer display.

1. To change the monitor settings to make the screen easier to read in safe mode, follow the appropriate step for your version of Windows:

- **Windows XP:** Choose Start⇨Control Panel to open the Control Panel window, and double-click the Display icon to open the Display Properties dialog box.

Alternatively, you can right-click the desktop and choose Properties from the shortcut menu.

- **Vista:** Choose Start⇨Control Panel.

- **Windows 7:** Choose Start⇨Control Panel⇨ Appearance and Personalization and then click Display to open the Display dialog box.

2. Again, follow the appropriate step for your version of Windows:

- **Windows XP and Vista:** On the Settings tab, select Screen Resolution and Color Quality settings that work properly with your system, and click OK.

- **Windows 7:** Select the Medium or Larger radio button (see **Figure 17-3**), and click the Apply button.

In Windows 7, you can right-click the desktop and choose Screen Resolution from the shortcut menu to adjust resolution, but you can't change color settings or themes in safe mode.

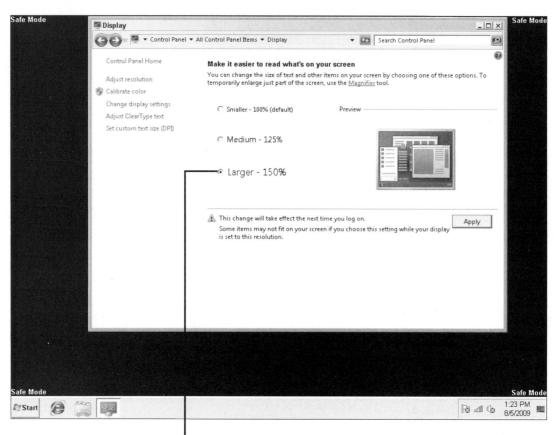

Choose a level of magnification.

Figure 17-3

Use Safe Mode Tools

When you've restarted a troublesome computer in safe mode, you can use several diagnostic and repair tools to attempt a fix. (Slight variations in operation may occur among Windows XP, Vista, and Windows 7.) Here are some of the most valuable tools:

➡ **Plug and play:** The availability of plug and play means that the computer can recognize most devices that are plugged in during or after start-up. Not all device drivers are available in safe mode, however. For more information on working with device drivers, see Chapter 4.

➡ **Help and Support:** Choose Start⇨Help and Support to open the Help and Support window, which provides searchable instructions and troubleshooting tips for many elements of the system (see **Figure 17-4**). In basic safe mode, however, networking and Internet access are disabled; to search on the Web for assistance, you have to choose the Safe Mode with Networking option during start-up (see "Choose Advanced Safe Mode Options," later in this chapter).

➡ **Device Manager:** This tool allows you to update device drivers and configure hardware. For details on using Device Manager, see Chapter 18.

➡ **System Restore:** This utility lets you retrieve settings and other information stored in the computer at an earlier time. I cover System Restore in detail in Chapter 16.

➡ **Command prompt:** In certain circumstances — such as when a support professional tells you to do so — you may want to reach the command prompt to run a program that resides outside Windows. To display the prompt (see **Figure 17-5**), choose Start⇨All Programs⇨Accessories⇨Command Prompt. Also see "Choose Advanced Safe Mode Options," later in this chapter, for more information.

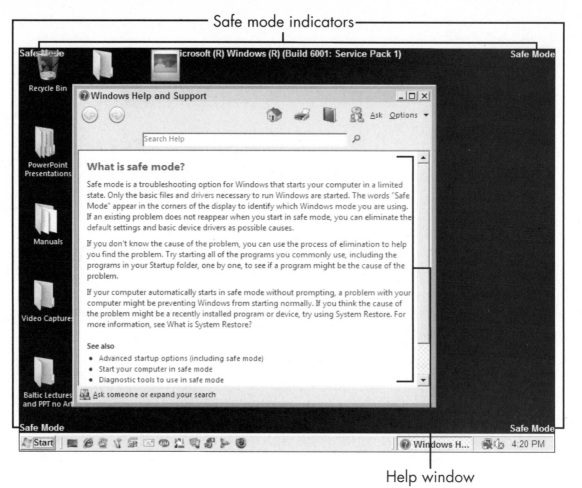

Safe mode indicators

Help window

Figure 17-4

➡ **Registry Editor:** This tool is not for inexperienced or unguided users. You may need to use it, however, if a support professional directs you to make changes in your Windows Registry files. Follow his or her instructions carefully.

 Don't make changes without backing up the previous set of files and without getting specific instructions about changes. A mistake in a critical section can render Windows unusable, requiring you to reinstall it.

Type commands at the command prompt.

Figure 17-5

Test New Hardware in Safe Mode

1. Start your computer in safe mode, as described earlier in this chapter.

2. Uninstall any drivers or other software that you installed for the new hardware. (See Chapter 4 for information on uninstalling programs and working with drivers.)

3. Choose Start⇨Shut Down to shut down the computer.

4. Uninstall the new hardware.

5. Restart the computer in normal mode.

6. If the problem goes away, you've isolated its source. Contact the manufacturer of the new hardware for assistance.

Test Settings in Safe Mode

1. Follow the appropriate step for your version of Windows:

➡ **Windows XP:** Choose Start⇨Control Panel to open the Control Panel window, and double-click the Display icon to open the Display Properties dialog box.

➡ **Vista and Windows 7:** Choose Start⇨Control Panel to open the Control Panel window. Then (in Classic View) click Display or (in Category View) select Appearance and Personalization and then click Display to open the Display dialog box.

2. Again, follow the appropriate step for your version of Windows:

➡ **Windows XP:** On the Settings tab, restore the resolution and color settings that were in effect before you started having problems, and click OK.

➡ **Vista and Windows 7:** Click Adjust Resolution, make the necessary changes, and click OK.

In Windows 7, you can't adjust color settings in safe mode, but you can adjust screen resolution.

Other system settings, such as network and soundcard configuration, aren't available in standard safe mode. See the next section for more options.

Choose Advanced Safe Mode Options

1. Follow Steps 1–4 of "Start Your Computer in Safe Mode," earlier in this chapter. In Windows XP and Vista, you see the Windows Advanced Options Menu screen; in Windows 7, you see the Advanced Boot Options Menu screen.

2. Use the arrow keys to select the option you want to use:

 In Windows 7 and Vista, a brief description appears at the bottom of the screen as you select each option.

- **Repair Your Computer (Vista and Windows 7 only):** This option displays a list of system-recovery options, including tools you can use to diagnose your current problems. You'll be asked to log in, after which you see a dialog box.

 If you don't see this dialog box, it may mean that your computer's manufacturer has supplied tools to replace these Microsoft utilities. Also, you may find these tools on your Windows CD but not on your hard drive.

- **Safe Mode:** This option (covered earlier in this chapter) loads Windows with a minimal set of drivers and services, permitting access to Control Panel and certain other utilities.

- **Safe Mode with Networking:** This option loads Windows in safe mode and also includes the standard set of drivers and services that you need to access the Internet or other computers on a network.

- **Safe Mode with Command Prompt:** This option loads Windows in safe mode but displays the command-prompt window instead of the usual Windows interface, permitting direct use of utilities that run outside Windows.

- **Enable Boot Logging:** During the start-up process, this option creates a file listing all the drivers that load during start-up. Examining the file, which is called `ntbtlog.txt`, may offer clues for advanced troubleshooting.

- **Enable VGA Mode (Windows XP and Vista) or Enable Low Resolution Video (Windows 7):** This option loads Windows with the current video driver but with low-resolution, minimal settings. This option allows you to reset the display settings if they were intentionally or accidentally set outside the acceptable range for your hardware.

- **Last Known Good Configuration:** This option loads Windows with the last configuration that worked successfully. I cover it in detail in Chapter 16.

- **Directory Services Restore Mode:** This advanced option is for system administrators and advanced users, but a support professional may direct you to choose it. This option loads the Windows domain controller running Active Directory so that the directory service can be restored. You wouldn't choose this option except under the direction of a Windows support professional.

- **Debugging Mode:** This option loads another advanced troubleshooting mode that lets you change certain elements of the Windows code itself. A support professional may direct you to choose this option, but don't enter this mode by yourself.

- **Disable Automatic Restart on System Failure:** This option (see **Figure 17-6**) allows you to specify whether Windows will restart automatically if an error causes it to fail. Microsoft recommends that you disable automatic restart if Windows is stuck in a loop in which it fails, attempts to restart, and fails again repeatedly.

- **Disable Driver Signature Enforcement (Vista and Windows 7 only):** This option allows drivers that contain improper or unverified signatures to be loaded.

- **Start Windows Normally:** This option, unlike the others in this menu, starts Windows in normal mode.

- **Recovery Console (Windows XP) or View System Recovery Options (Vista):** Choose this option to display a menu of recovery options that can help you solve problems related to start-up.

Disable automatic restart if Windows cycles and won't start up properly.

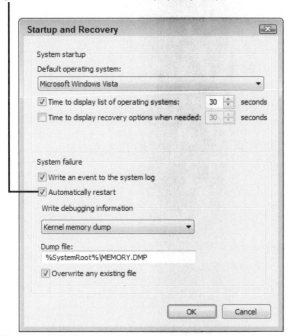

Figure 17-6

System Recovery Options is a suite of recovery and repair tools. You see this option only if these utilities have been installed on your hard drive. Otherwise, you can find them on your Vista CD. Depending on your computer brand, the manufacturer may have substituted another utility for this one.

- **Reboot:** This option lets you restart the system. Unless you press the F8 key to start in safe mode, this option restarts the computer normally.

- **Return to OS Choices Menu:** If your computer contains more than one version of Windows, this option returns you to the start-up menu so you can choose which version you want to launch.

3. Press Enter to start Windows in the selected mode.

Exit Safe Mode

1. Restart the computer from the Start menu.

2. Allow Windows to load normally.

Part V

Troubleshooting Your PC

The 5th Wave   By Rich Tennant

©RICHTENNANT

"We're much better prepared for this upgrade than before. We're giving users additional training, better manuals, and a morphine drip."

Managing and Troubleshooting Devices

Device Manager, a key component of the System utility in Control Panel, is a full-time, officially licensed internal snoop and reporter. As its name tells you, its assignment is to manage the devices that do the work.

In addition, this utility gives you a window on the various hardware components that make up your computer. Here, devices are grouped according to their function. You can retrieve device names, view driver information, find out whether a device is working properly, enable or disable a device, and more. Device Manager is a valuable tool that helps you understand more about your computer system and troubleshoot hardware problems.

In this chapter, I show you how to use Device Manager to keep your system running smoothly — and how to troubleshoot device problems if you need more help.

See What You Can Do with Device Manager

➠ View a list of the devices installed in your computer system. **Figure** 18-1 shows a sample list in Device Manager. (Your computer's list will be similar but certainly not the same.)

Click a plus sign (+) to expand any device category.

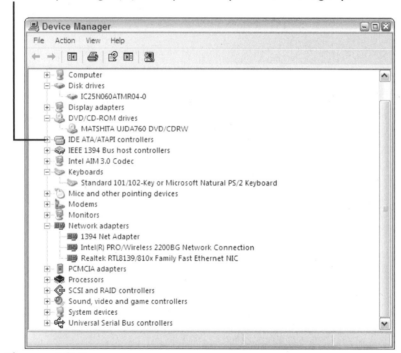

Figure 18-1

➠ Temporarily disable any listed device to help with a troubleshooting process (see "Disable a Device," later in this chapter). If your PC works properly with a single device disabled, either that device is causing the problem, or it's in conflict with another device (see "Resolve a Conflict," later in this chapter).

➠ See at a glance whether the system has found problems, such as malfunctioning hardware or intermittent device conflicts.

➠ Get data about the microprocessor and other major components of the motherboard.

➠ See information about many external devices that are in continuous communication with your computer.

➠ Print a report on the status of your devices.

➠ Examine the resources (including memory) that any device uses.

➠ View details on the drivers for each device, including the publisher of the software and its version name or number.

➠ Update, roll back, or uninstall device drivers.

 If Windows was set up on your PC with an Administrator account (most often done in offices, where one person or department is in charge of managing multiple computers), you have to sign in as the administrator to manage devices and make certain changes in settings.

Open Device Manager

1. Follow the appropriate step for your version of Windows:

• **Windows XP:** Choose Start⇨Control Panel to open the Control Panel window; double-click the System icon to display the System Properties dialog box; click the Hardware tab; and then click the Device Manager button (see **Figure 18-2**).

• **Vista and Windows 7:** Choose Start⇨Control Panel to open the Control Panel window. Then (in Classic View) click Device Manager or (in Category View) click Hardware and Sound to open the Hardware and Sound dialog box; then click Device Manager in the Devices and Printers section.

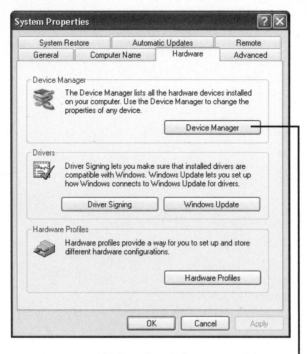

Click to launch Device Manager.

Figure 18-2

Whichever method you use, Device Manager opens.

2. Check the Device Manager window for any warning icons. If Device Manager has detected a problem, it displays either of two warning icons next to the device in question:

- **An exclamation point (!) in a yellow circle** indicates a potential or actual conflict (see **Figure 18-3**). See the next section, "Resolve a Conflict," for information on what to do next.

- **An X in a red circle** tells you that a device is disabled — physically installed on your computer but not functioning. Either you've disabled the device (see "Disable a Device," later in this chapter), or a troubleshooting utility has disabled it for you.

3. Double-click the name of a device or category to display its properties. You can double-click the Processors entry, for example, to find out what kind of processor your computer uses.

 To display individual devices in a category, click the plus sign (+) (Windows XP) or the right-pointing arrow (Vista and Windows 7).

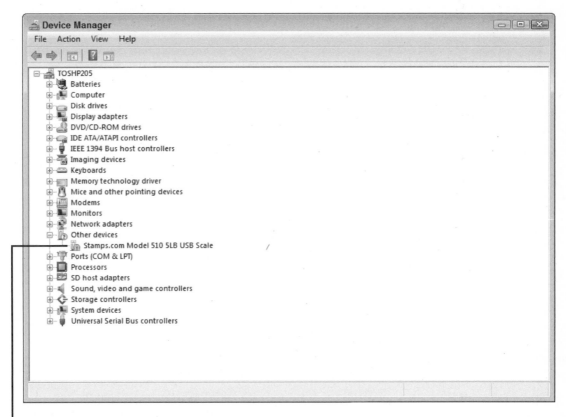

This icon indicates a possible conflict involving this device

Figure 18-3

4. Click the Driver tab to view information about the driver software installed to support this device.

 If you click the Driver Details button in this dialog box, Windows displays the path to the device's drivers. For information on updating drivers, see "Update a Device Driver," later in this chapter.

Resolve a Conflict

1. Double-click any device with a warning icon (see "Open Device Manager," earlier in this chapter) to display its Properties dialog box.

2. Click the General tab, and read the Device Status section (**Figure 18-4**). This section may list specific information about the nature of any problem; you can use those details to change configurations by yourself or with the assistance of a support technician.

3. If the Device Status section reports that the device is working properly, proceed to Step 4.

or

If the Device Status section reports that the device isn't working properly, click the Troubleshoot button, and skip to "Use a Windows Troubleshooting Wizard," later in this chapter.

4. If the device uses system resources, you should find a Resources tab in the Properties dialog box; click that tab.

5. Check the Conflicting Device List section at the bottom of the Resources tab. This information may be sufficient to help you figure out which device needs to be reconfigured or replaced. **Figure 18-5** shows this section for a device that has no conflicts.

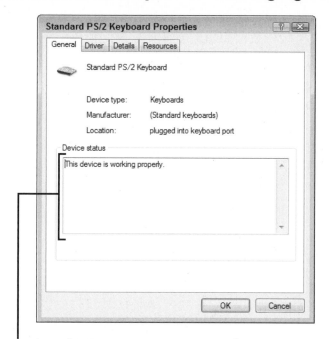

Look in the Device Status section for details on problems with this device.

Figure 18-4

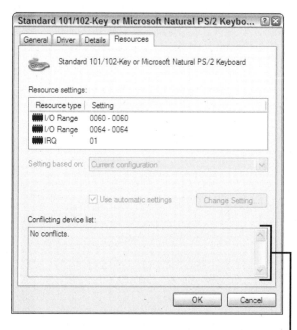

Look here for possible device conflicts.

Figure 18-5

Disable a Device

 Disabling a device (actually, disabling its device driver and its request for use of system resources) can be very helpful in tracking down the source of a problem with your computer or with Windows. When a potentially problematic device is disabled, you can see status reports and error messages that may assist you.

1. Launch Device Manager (see "Open Device Manager," earlier in this chapter).

2. Click the plus sign (+) next to the device's category to expand the listing (see **Figure 18-6**).

3. Double-click the device that you want to disable. The device's Properties dialog box opens.

4. Follow the appropriate step for your version of Windows:

- **Windows XP and Vista:** Click the General tab. In the Device Usage section at the bottom of the tab, choose Do Not Use This Device (Disable) from the drop-down menu (see **Figure 18-7**).

- **Windows 7:** Click the Driver tab, and choose Disable at the bottom of the tab.

 The wording of the disable option may differ slightly in various versions of Windows, but the effect is the same.

5. Click OK to apply the change and close the dialog box.

6. If you don't see an immediate change in your computer's operation, restart your PC to allow all the installed devices to make their presences known to Device Manager.

Expanded category

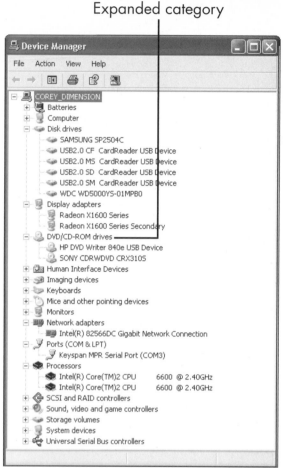

Figure 18-6

 For external devices that connect to the system through a USB port, you can achieve the same effect by unplugging the device from the computer or (if it draws its own power from a wall socket) turning off its switch. If the device includes memory, however, you should first click the Safely Remove Hardware icon at the right end of the taskbar and choose the device from the pop-up menu. To remove a USB storage device in Windows 7, choose Start➪Devices and Printers, right-click the device in the Devices and Printers window, and choose Eject from the shortcut menu.

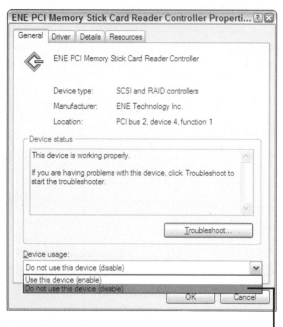

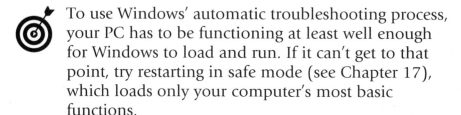

Enable and disable devices with this menu.
Figure 18-7

Use a Windows Troubleshooting Wizard

To use Windows' automatic troubleshooting process, your PC has to be functioning at least well enough for Windows to load and run. If it can't get to that point, try restarting in safe mode (see Chapter 17), which loads only your computer's most basic functions.

1. Launch Device Manager (see "Open Device Manager," earlier in this chapter).

2. Click the plus sign next to the category you want to troubleshoot to expand the list of items in that category.

3. Right-click the troubled device, and choose Properties from the shortcut menu to open the device's Properties dialog box.

4. Click the General tab, and read the information listed in the Device Status section, which may tell you the nature of the problem and suggest a solution.

5. To get help, click the Troubleshoot button. Windows Help and Support Center launches a troubleshooting wizard for the device in question (see **Figure 18-8**).

Select your problem, and click Next.

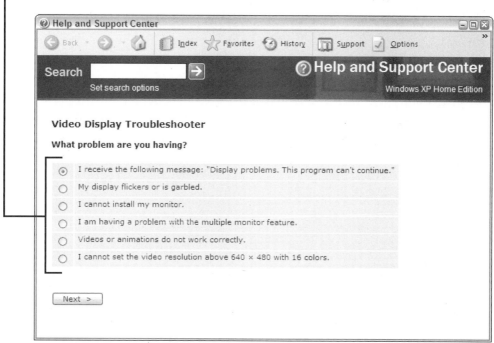

Figure 18-8

6. Follow the wizard's instructions, being sure to click the Next button at the bottom of each wizard screen to proceed to the next step.

Update a Device Driver

1. Launch Device Manager (see "Open Device Manager," earlier in this chapter).

2. Click the plus sign next to the category you want to troubleshoot to expand the list of items in that category.

3. Right-click the troubled device, and choose Properties from the shortcut menu to open the device's Properties dialog box.

4. Click the Driver tab.

5. Click Update Driver to launch the Hardware Update Wizard (Windows XP) or the Update Driver Software dialog box (Vista and Windows 7).

6. Select Yes when Windows asks permission to connect to Windows Update to look for a driver (XP). In Vista and Windows 7 the search will be begin as soon as you click the automatic search choice on the update screen.

7. Click Next (XP) to display an action summary screen, then click Next again to accept the automatic installation option.

8. Follow any onscreen instructions. If Windows determines that your driver is current, it displays a notice to that effect; otherwise, it proceeds to install the current driver.

9. If you're installing a new driver in an attempt to solve a problem, restart your computer after installation, and test the problem device.

 It's a good idea to set a new restore point before installing new software so that you can revert to the earlier configuration if necessary. For details, see Chapter 16.

Relieving Hard Times for Hard Drives

The hard disk drive in your computer is a mechanical device, kind of like a lawn-mower, a food processor, or a record player (remember those?). Like all mechanical devices, it has a limited life expectancy.

If you're unlucky, your drive will die suddenly. If you're lucky, it will break down slowly over a long period. Make no mistake, though: Someday, your hard drive *will* die. That's why it's important to check its health regularly and keep it in the best possible shape.

You can do several things to check and maintain your drive:

⟹ Use an automated maintenance utility provided by the drive maker or a third-party software company

⟹ Perform a manual check with maintenance tools that are built into Windows

⟹ Defragment the drive

⟹ Check for disk errors

The one thing you should *not* do is ignore any developing issue.

In this chapter, I show you how to tune up your hard drive and keep it running as long as possible.

Defragment the Drive with Windows' Defragmenting Tool

1. Choose Start⇨All Programs⇨Accessories⇨System Tools⇨ Disk Defragmenter to display the Disk Defragmenter dialog box (see **Figure 19-1**).

Click here for more information.

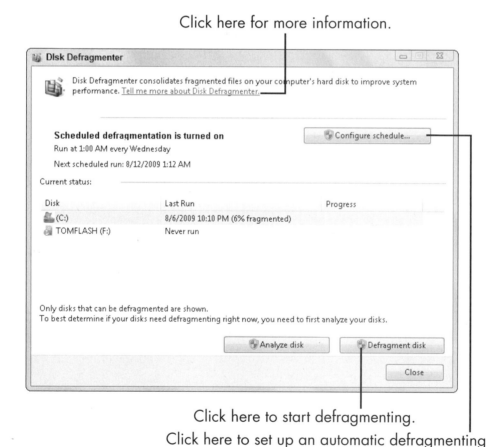

Click here to start defragmenting.

Click here to set up an automatic defragmenting schedule in Vista and Windows 7.

Figure 19-1

2. Select the drive that you want to defragment.

 For most users, the main hard drive is designated the C: drive; it contains Windows, your applications, and your data. This drive has the most storage. You may also see a much smaller D: drive, which likely contains the files you would use to restore your computer to factory settings in the event of a problem. You don't want to alter anything on this recovery drive.

3. Click Defragment (Windows XP) or Defragment Disk (Vista and Windows 7). The defragmenter analyzes the disk for degree of fragmentation and then begins the defragmentation process.

In Windows XP, you see a graphical display that represents the hard drive before and after defragmentation. In Vista and Windows 7, you see a countdown of the percentage of defragmentation completed.

4. When the process is complete, close Disk Defragmenter by choosing File⇨Exit (Windows XP) or by clicking the Close button (Vista and Windows 7).

 In Windows 7 and Vista, you can configure Disk Defragmenter to run on a schedule, which keeps your hard drive tuned up and efficient without your having to think about it.

 Don't allow your drives to become so full that a defragmentation tool — either the built-in Windows tool or a third-party product (see the next section) — has little or no room to rearrange files. In most cases, you shouldn't fill a drive to more than 85 percent of its capacity; that means leaving at least 15 percent available for the utility. Delete junk or move some files to external storage if you need to open space.

Defragment the Drive with a Third-Party Utility

Why spend money for a tool that does the same thing as Disk Defragmenter? Third-party defraggers provide extra bells and whistles that may be worth paying for. Here are a few of the best third-party defragmentation utilities:

➟ Norton 360 and Norton Systemworks (www.symantec.com)

➟ Diskeeper Professional (www.diskeeper.com; see **Figure 19-2**)

Color-coded defragmentation analysis

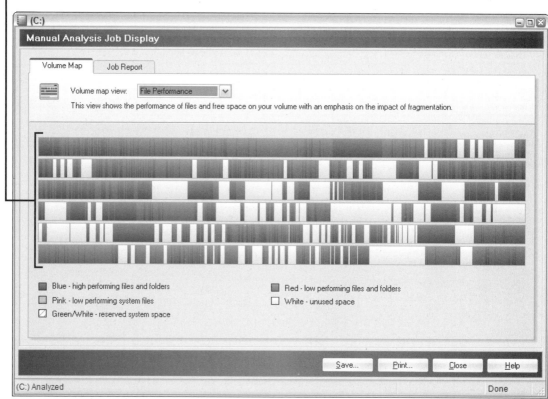

Figure 19-2

If you use a scheduled defragmentation tool such as the one built into Windows 7 (as opposed to one that works in the background, like the Norton products and Diskeeper), you'll get better and faster results if you turn off your computer's Internet connection while the program is running. Otherwise, new e-mail and other automatic activities that bring files to your computer will slow the process — sometimes to the point at which the tool has to start all over again.

Check for Disk Errors Automatically

1. Choose Start⇨My Computer or Start⇨Computer to open the My Computer/Computer window.

2. Right-click the drive you want to check, and choose Properties from the shortcut menu to open the drive's Properties dialog box.

3. Check the General tab for information about your drive, such as total capacity and free space (see **Figure 19-3**). A drive that is 99 percent full may not report errors, but it may act like it has hardware problems. If so, delete some files to make more room.

4. Click the Tools tab, and click the Check Now button. The Check Disk dialog box opens (see **Figure 19-4**).

5. Select one or both of the following options:

- **Automatically Fix File System Errors:** If this box is checked, the utility will examine all the files, folders, and indexes on the drive and repair most basic problems that it finds.

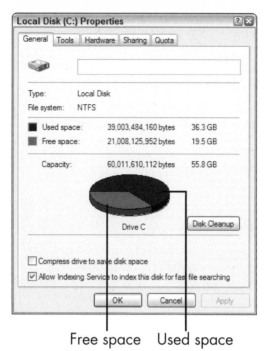

Free space   Used space

Figure 19-3

Choose your options, and click
Start to scan for errors.

Figure 19-4

- **Scan for and Attempt Recovery of Bad Sectors:** If
  this box is checked, the utility will examine the
  magnetic sector markings on the surface of the

disk, looking for any that are corrupted, incorrect, or damaged. If possible, the utility will repair damaged sector marking. If that portion of the disk is damaged, the utility may be able to place an electronic fence around the sector so that your PC doesn't attempt to place new information there.

6. Click the Start button to begin the scan. If you selected the automatic-check option in Step 5, Windows displays a message that the check can't be performed while you're using the disk and asks whether you want the utility to check the disk the next time you restart your PC.

7. Follow the appropriate step for your version of Windows:

- **Windows XP:** Click Yes to tell Windows to check your disk at the next restart.

- **Vista and Windows 7:** Click Schedule Disk Check.

 If your Vista or Windows 7 computer is set up to have an administrator perform certain functions, you'll be asked to enter an administrator password at this point. Most home and small-business PCs, however, aren't set up to be managed by an administrator.

If you chose Scan for and Attempt Recovery of Bad Sectors in Step 5, you can continue to work on your computer, if you want, while the test is under way. You can get some idea of the status of the checkup by watching the slow advance of the progress bars onscreen, but don't expect a play-by-play report.

At the end of the scan, Windows will report whether or not errors were found and corrected. If you opted to schedule an automatic check on the next restart,

Windows reports that a disk check has been scheduled, gives you a chance to cancel, and then goes about running the Check Disk utility.

You don't have to check for disk errors every day, but you should do it every few months or whenever you notice erratic behavior that may be disk-related.

Check for Disk Errors Manually with Chkdsk

This method takes a side trip out of Windows into the dark recesses of the command prompt — the mostly hidden vestige of the PC's ancestral operating system — via a utility called Chkdsk. This text-based utility will be familiar to old-time computer users. Welcome to the past.

1. Follow the appropriate step for your version of Windows:

- **Windows XP:** Choose Start⇨Run to display the dialog box, type **cmd** in the Open text box, and click OK.

- **Vista:** Click the Start button, type **cmd** in the Search Programs and Files field, and press Enter. Windows opens a dialog box displaying the message `This task will be created with Administrative privileges.` Click OK.

- **Windows 7:** Click the Start button, type **cmd** in the Search Programs and Files field, and press Enter. Right-click cmd in the search-results window, and choose Run as Administrator from the shortcut menu. When Windows asks permission to make changes in User Access Control, click Yes.

Whichever method you use, the command-prompt window opens.

 You won't be able to work on your computer while this utility is running.

2. Enter one of the following commands:

- To view detailed information about your hard drive, type **chkdsk** *driveletter*: and then press Enter. (You enter the drive letter in place of *driveletter*. To check drive C:, for example, type the command **chkdsk c:**.)

- To find and repair errors, locate bad sectors, and recover readable information that may have been lost to an application, type **chkdsk** *driveletter*:/r and then press Enter. (Substitute the actual drive letter for *driveletter*. To check drive C:, for example, type **chkdsk c:/r**.)

Programs such as chkdsk can be executed (run) with command switches that tell the program to conduct special tasks. You enter a switch after the program name, preceded by a slash (/). The /r switch, for example, tells Chkdsk to find and repair errors.

If the current drive is in use (which is often the case in a PC that has just one drive), Chkdsk informs you that it can't run the test with the specified repairs now and offers to conduct it the next time the computer starts. Type **Y** (for yes) and then press Enter. The next time you start your computer, Chkdsk will run its test before Windows loads.

3. Wait for Chkdsk to finish doing its thing and display details on what it found (see **Figure 19-5**).

Result of a Chkdsk scan

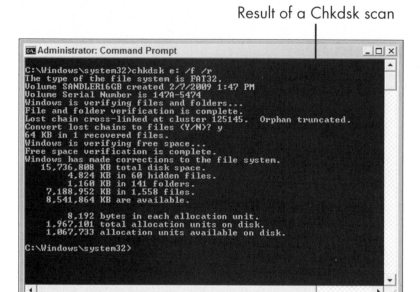

Figure 19-5

Here are the possibilities and their meanings:

Exit Code	Description
0	No errors were found.
1	Errors were found and fixed.
2	Disk cleanup, such as garbage collection, was performed, or cleanup wasn't performed because the /f switch wasn't specified. (/f is the error-fix switch that's included in the /r switch, which I discuss earlier in this section.)
3	Chkdsk couldn't check the disk or couldn't fix errors because the /f switch wasn't specified.

4. What you do next depends on the result of the test. If you asked Chkdsk to fix errors, for example, it may display an exit code or ask for verification before it performs a repair or recovery task. To continue the process, type **Y** and then press Enter.

5. Type **exit** and press Enter to close the command-prompt window.

 Again, if Windows is using one or more of the files on the hard drive, you see the following message: Chkdsk cannot run because the volume is in use by another process. Would you like to schedule this volume to be checked the next time the system restarts? (Y/N) Type **Y** and press Enter to schedule the disk check; then restart your computer.

Take Out the Garbage with Disk Cleanup

1. Choose Start➪My Computer or Start➪My Computer to open the My Computer/Computer window.

2. Right-click the drive you want to check, and choose Properties from the shortcut menu to open the drive's Properties dialog box (refer to Figure 19-3, earlier in this chapter).

3. Click the General tab, if it isn't already open.

4. If you want, check the Compress This Drive to Save Disk Space check box. This option compresses old files that you haven't used for a while.

 Choosing the Compress option generally is a good idea, although some users (including me) would rather not touch older files and compensate by adding more storage. (See Chapter 11 for details on adding or replacing a hard drive.)

5. Click the Disk Cleanup button. The system churns away for a while, examining your drive and calculating how much garbage it can locate.

Finally, the Disk Cleanup dialog box opens (see **Figure 19-6**), indicating how much junk is sitting around in places like the folders for downloaded program files, temporary Internet files, and the Recycle Bin, and suggesting files to delete.

Disk space that will be recovered
if you delete these files

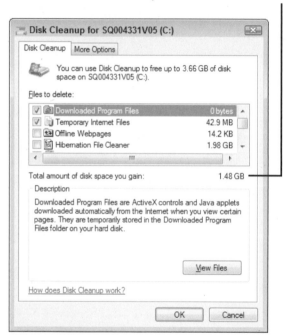

Figure 19-6

6. Clear the check boxes next to any files that you want to keep; check the check boxes next to any additional files that you want to clear off the disk.

 For most users, it's best to delete only the recommended files. If you choose to go further, click each file and read its description before proceeding.

7. Click OK.

8. When Windows asks you to confirm that you want to delete these files permanently, click Yes (Windows XP) or Delete Files (Vista and Windows 7).

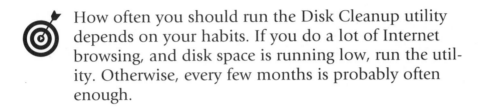 How often you should run the Disk Cleanup utility depends on your habits. If you do a lot of Internet browsing, and disk space is running low, run the utility. Otherwise, every few months is probably often enough.

Fixing Common Problems

As Claude Rains advised in *Casablanca*, when things go awry, the first thing to do is round up the usual suspects. The same is true for computers. Although there are uncountable possible combinations of hardware, software, and settings, most problems can be traced to a relatively small number of causes.

In this chapter, I give you tips for troubleshooting some of the most common PC problems.

Start a Computer That Won't Start

1. Check the computer's power source and connections.

- Make certain that the power cord is plugged into the computer *and* into a source of power. The power cord runs from the back of the computer and plugs into an electrical socket in the wall; into a surge protector (a good thing); or (even better) into an uninterruptible power supply (*UPS*), which is basically a large battery that is continuously recharged by wall current (see **Figure 20-1**).

Figure 20-1

- Test the source of power to see whether it's live. To do that, plug a lamp, radio, or fan into the same outlet, surge protector, or UPS that you're using for your computer, and see whether that device works properly. If not, the wall outlet may have blown a fuse or the surge protector may have failed (which is its job if a power spike comes along). For more details on dealing with a power problem, see Chapter 9.

- Try an alternative source of power, such as a different wall socket. Then turn the computer back on and hope for a return to normalcy.

2. Push the start button or click the power switch, and listen for the computer's cooling fan. A silent machine plugged into a live power outlet may indicate a failure in the power supply or circuitry. For details on replacing a failed power supply (or directing a technician to do it for you), see Chapter 9.

3. Listen and watch for beeps, other alert tones, or flashing lights on the front panel after the PC's fan comes to life. These alerts during start-up (your computer's instruction manual may explain them) may indicate a problem with internal hardware, such as memory or the hard disk drive. If you need to replace hardware, turn to Part III.

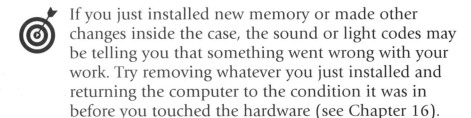 If you just installed new memory or made other changes inside the case, the sound or light codes may be telling you that something went wrong with your work. Try removing whatever you just installed and returning the computer to the condition it was in before you touched the hardware (see Chapter 16).

4. Watch for onscreen messages before Windows is loaded. These messages could warn you of a hardware failure or an error resulting from a problem with setup instructions.

Sometimes, you can get past a hardware error by instructing Windows to open in safe mode (see Chapter 17), which loads only the most critical components of Windows. If Windows will load this way, you can check Device Manager for clues about which component failed; for details, see Chapter 18.

Solve Basic Hardware Problems

➡ **Your computer is suddenly silent.** Make sure you haven't muted the sound. The sound card or adapter inside your PC has failed or is no longer adequate for your needs.

Solution: Instead of opening the case, plug in an external sound adapter such as Creative's USB SoundBlaster Live! 24-Bit External, which attaches to a USB port on almost any desktop or laptop computer.

➡ **Your PC needs new or better wireless capability.** You want to give your computer the ability to communicate wirelessly with other devices, or you need to upgrade an outdated or malfunctioning built-in Wi-Fi adapter.

Solution: Several manufacturers offer external Wi-Fi adapters and antennas that connect to your PC through (you're getting the pattern here, right?) the USB port. One advantage of using an external Wi-Fi adapter is that it usually comes with a more substantial antenna than its internal equivalent, and you can adjust the placement of that antenna to get the best transmission and reception in your home or office. The latest "N" Wi-Fi technology adapters, like the one shown in **Figure 20-2,** have a small footprint and offer better coverage than earlier models do.

Figure 20-2

➡ **You can't install programs on a computer with no CD/DVD drive.** If you own a minimalist netbook or a small desktop computer, the tiny size and low cost often come at the expense of things like a CD/DVD drive. But without a CD/DVD drive, how do you install new programs?

Solution: A couple of simple work-arounds are available:

- **Use the Internet.** The first and most obvious solution is to download programs or data over the Internet or across a local area network, or to use a device such as a flash memory drive to transfer program content to the computer. You can purchase very large flash drives to store up to 256GB worth of programs or data. **Figure 20-3**, for example, shows a Kingston 128GB USB flash drive. Old-timers like me find it hard to believe that you can get so much storage in such a small package.

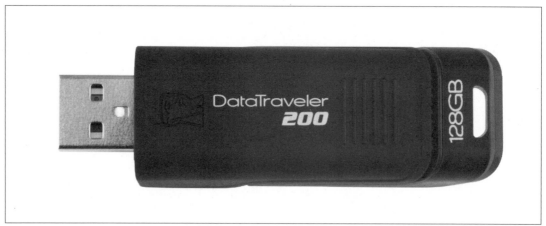

Figure 20-3

- **Install an external CD/DVD drive.** Another option is to install an external drive. Drives of this type are small units, similar to those used in full-feature laptops, that draw electrical power from wall current and connect to the computer through the USB port. (For details on external drives, see Chapter 11.) **Figure 20-4** shows a typical external CD/DVD drive that can read and write discs.

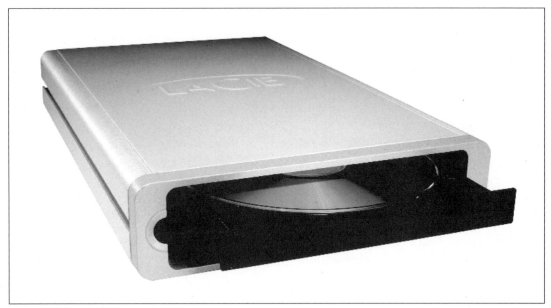

Figure 20-4

 For information on fixing other hardware glitches, see Part III.

Troubleshoot Common Windows Woes

➡ **Windows is damaged.** The version of Windows installed on your PC has become damaged, and your only option seems to be a clean reinstallation. First consider which applications you really need to keep and use after this process; then make sure that you have the original installation discs for these programs.

Solution: Follow these steps:

1. Plug in an external hard drive as an additional storage device. If the drive has been formatted and includes any data (virtually all modern drives are configured for plug-and-play installation), Windows will ask your intentions (see **Figure 20-5**).

Select an option if necessary, and click OK.

Figure 20-5

2. If the drive is new, all you want to do is make it available to Windows, so you don't need to select an option; simply click OK.

3. Use Windows Explorer to copy all your data from the internal drive to the external drive.

4. Repartition and reformat the internal drive, and reinstall Windows (all covered in Chapter 11).

5. Restart your PC.

6. When Windows is up and running properly, copy your data files on the external drive back to the internal drive.

7. Reinstall any applications that you want to use. (Unfortunately, when you reformat a drive and reinstall Windows, you lose your other applications.)

 You may want to keep the external drive attached and use it to store backup copies of your data files.

➠ **After you install a new program, Windows stops working properly.** The new program may be incompatible with your version of Windows. Restart Windows in safe mode, uninstall the program, and then contact the manufacturer to see whether it offers a later version of the program (or a patch that makes it compatible with your version of Windows). For more information on safe mode, see Chapter 17; for details on uninstalling software, turn to Chapter 4.

➠ **After you install a new piece of hardware, Windows no longer works properly.** The most likely culprit is a device driver that's incompatible with your version of Windows or that conflicts with a driver for a different piece of hardware. Try uninstalling and reinstalling the driver, and check for a new version that may be more compatible with your system. For details on checking for device conflicts, see Chapter 18.

 For full coverage of Windows issues, see Part IV.

Solve Basic Software Problems

➠ **After you install a new program or change your Windows settings, your computer freezes.** Evidently, the new software has something to do with the problem.

Solution: Try restarting the PC to see whether the problem goes away after restart. If not, use System Restore (see Chapter 16) to return your computer to the configuration it was in before you made the change. **Figure 20-6** shows the System Restore screen in which you choose which restore point to use.

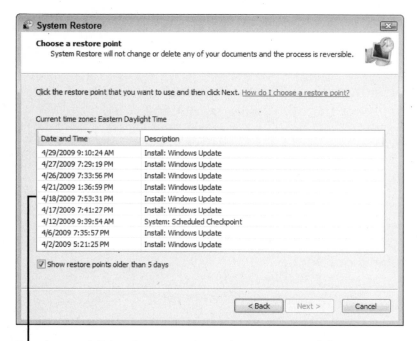

Send your PC back in time by selecting one of these restore points.
Figure 20-6

Another option is to restart your computer in safe mode, undo your most recent changes in Control Panel, restart again, and allow Windows to load normally. For more information, see "Undo Something You Just Did" in Chapter 16.

➠ **An application that once worked is reporting problems or isn't running at all.** A few misplaced bits of program data due to a hard drive problem or program conflict can cause applications to lose their minds, so to speak. You could be experiencing a hardware failure (see "Solve Basic Hardware Problems," earlier in this chapter), a problem with Windows (see "Troubleshoot Common Windows Woes," earlier in this chapter), or issues between the application and Windows.

Solution: Try these fixes:

- If the program will open, and you can access its menus, look for a software-update option (probably in the File or Help menu). Windows conducts periodic automatic updates unless you've disabled this feature. An older application could resist a major Windows update by refusing to run properly.

- If you can't find an update option in any menus, check the manufacturer's Web site, where you may be able to download and install the latest software version.

- Remove the program; then reinstall it from the original discs. See Chapter 4 for details on how to uninstall a program.

Get Back on the Internet

1. Let Windows help you solve the problem.

- If you attempt to connect to a Web page and get a message similar to the one shown in **Figure 20-7**, click More Information for help.

- Click Diagnose Connection Problems.

Click for more information.

Click to let Windows try to solve your problem.

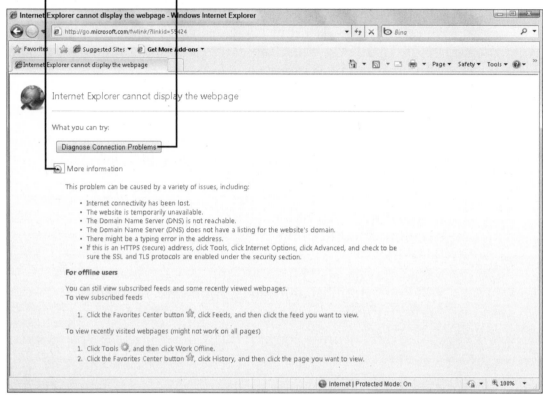

Figure 20-7

 You may see slightly different responses to a bad Internet connection, depending on the browser you're using.

2. Make sure that your Internet connection is still active. If you have a cable or DSL modem, an indicator light should tell you whether the service is active.

  • **Cable modem:** If you use a cable modem, also check to see whether any television sets connected to the line are getting a video signal.

- **DSL modem:** If you use a DSL modem, see whether any telephones attached to the line have a dial tone.

If your service seems to be working properly, the problem may be caused by a momentary electrical glitch in the signal that can lock up the modem. Proceed to Step 3.

3. Try a power reset, as follows:

   a. Close your Web browser and other programs on your computer.

   b. Remove the power cord from the modem (and, if you use one, from the router).

   c. Wait about 10 seconds.

   d. Restore the power to the modem (and router, if applicable), and wait until all the indicator lights come back on.

   e. Open your Web browser, and see whether Internet access has been restored.

4. If you still don't have Internet access, and the modem indicator light still shows problems, call your Internet service provider's support desk for assistance.

If the support person tries to avoid helping you — perhaps by claiming that the problem is in the internal wiring of your home or office, or that your computer is malfunctioning or improperly configured — insist that he or she help you solve the problem. One way to get the company's attention: Tell the support representative that you're prepared to cancel your service because you can't get the Internet to work, and ask to be connected to the billing department. All of a sudden, someone — often, a supervisor — will be made available to you to solve the problem.

5. If you still don't have Internet access after Step 3, but the modem's indicator light shows that the service is working properly, retrace your steps. Have you made any changes in Windows or installed any new programs since the last time your PC linked up properly to the Web? If so, restore the previous settings manually or with System Restore (see Chapter 16).

Glossary

application software: The program your computer uses to do work, such as a word processing or a spreadsheet program.

bandwidth: The amount of data that can be transmitted over an electronic line in a fixed amount of time. For digital devices, bandwidth is usually expressed in bits per second or bytes per second. For analog devices, bandwidth is expressed in cycles per second, or Hertz (Hz).

bank switching: A technology to expand available system memory by switching between banks of memory as needed. The off bank retains its memory when not in use but is not immediately available.

base memory: The amount of available memory for programs in the first megabyte of memory in a PC.

bit: The smallest piece of information in a computer represented as a 1 or a 0. A bit can represent a number or a state, such as ON or OFF, or TRUE or FALSE. A byte has eight bits.

bits per second: bps. The number of binary digits that can be transmitted in one second. A more accurate means of measuring the potential speed of a modem.

boot: The process the computer goes through to set itself up and load its operating system. Two kinds of boot exist: hard (or cold) and soft (or warm).

boot drive: The disk drive from where the operating system is loaded.

boot sector: The first sector of the active (bootable) partition.

broadband: A high-speed means of connection to the Internet, such as cable modem or DSL telephone wiring.

burn: The act of recording information onto an optical storage medium such as a CD-R or DVD-R. The device's unit burns pits, or markings, on the disc to indicate the 0s and 1s of digital data.

byte: Eight bits, the smallest unit of data moved about in a personal computer.

cache: Memory used to store multiple pieces of data that the computer can reasonably guess it will need soon.

CD-R: Compact Disc-Recordable. A family of devices that can write a permanent record to a special type of CD, which can then be read on a standard CD-ROM drive or another CD-R device. Also known as *Compact Disc-Writable.*

CD-ROM: Compact Disc Read-Only Memory. An adaptation of music CD technology that stores large amounts of data.

chip: A casual name for an integrated circuit. A chip is a silicon wafer that has layers of circuits photoetched into its silicon surface. Chip also refers to the ceramic or plastic packages in which chips come.

chipset: An integrated set of chips that performs the functions of a larger number of discrete logical devices on a PC.

cold boot: Starting or restarting a computer by removing all power to the system or pressing the reset button. Compare to warm boot. In certain situations, a cold boot is necessary to reset some hardware devices.

command prompt: A screen symbol from the operating system that indicates the system is awaiting input from the user — for example, C:>.

conventional memory: Memory located between 0 and 640K, separated by IBM PC convention from addresses above 640K to 1MB, and intended for use by the OS (operating system) and applications.

corruption: When data becomes scrambled, changed, or otherwise damaged.

CPU: The Central Processing Unit is the part of the computer that executes instructions and manipulates information. PCs are based on Intel or compatible CPUs, including the original 8088 and later chips, such as the 80286, 80386, 486, Pentium, Pentium MMX, Pentium II, Celeron, Pentium III, and Pentium 4.

debug: The process of finding and removing bugs, or errors, in a piece of software. From the very first PC through modern machines, the operating system has included a utility called DEBUG that allows advanced users to directly alter bytes of data in memory or in storage.

DRAM: Dynamic Random Access Memory. Memory chips that need to be refreshed regularly. DRAM temporarily stores data in a cell made up of a tiny capacitor and transistor.

DSL: Digital subscriber line. A DSL is a form of communication offered by telephone companies and third parties that permits broadband Internet connection. Although fast, DSL lines are usually surpassed by cable modem connections.

dual boot: A configuration that enables a computer to be loaded with more than one operating system, with the user able to choose among them at boot.

dual-core processor: *See* multicore processor.

DVD: Digital Video Disc or Digital Versatile Disc. A standard for high-density data, audio, and video. DVD is stored on a media the size of a compact disc.

Energy Star: A specification for power-saving designs.

expansion slot: A connector on the motherboard that allows an expansion card to electrically become part of the bus.

extended memory: The memory in a modern machine with an address above 1MB. It can be used under DOS by programs that throw the 286, 386, or 486 CPU chip — and advanced CPUs that emulate earlier microprocessors — into protected mode, where the CPU and associated programs can take advantage of this memory. Can be used to provide expanded memory.

external drive: A storage device that exists outside of the case of the PC, connected to it by a cable. Common interfaces for external devices include FireWire, parallel, SCSI, and USB.

firewall: A piece of software or a hardware device intended to block intruders from accessing computers attached to a local area network or the Internet.

FireWire: A fast and flexible external bus standard originally developed as the IEEE 1394 specification and later renamed by Apple as FireWire. In its current version it permits data transfer rates of as much as 400 Mbps, with faster versions expected.

flash disk: A storage device using flash memory. Examples include PC Card memory, CompactFlash, and Smart Media cards.

Gb: *See* gigabit.

GB: *See* gigabyte.

giga: One billion.

gigabit (Gb): Used informally to mean one billion bits of storage in hard drives and other storage media. For RAM, the actual size of a gigabit is 1,024 megabits, or 1,073,741,824 bits.

gigabyte (GB): Used informally to mean one billion bytes of storage in hard drives and other storage media. For RAM, the actual size of a gigabyte is 1,024 megabytes, or 1,073,741,824 bytes.

hard disk: A large-capacity storage medium that uses spinning platters coated with magnetic material.

hard reset: Instructing a running system to reboot by pressing a reset button on the hardware. Also known as a cold boot. Compare to *warm boot.*

heat sink: A metallic (often aluminum) structure with vanes that radiate heat away from a hot component, helping to prevent failure of electronic devices. Modern microprocessors require a heat sink, cooling fan, or both because of the amount of heat they produce.

HIMEM.SYS: A device driver that manages extended memory in DOS; Windows provides an equivalent as part of its internal code.

hot swapping: The ability to attach or detach a device to a computer while it is running, a feature that is one of the advantages of USB and FireWire systems.

inkjet printer: A printing device that creates text or images by spraying tiny dots onto a page.

internal drive: A storage device that mounts within the case of a PC. A floppy disk, CD-ROM, Zip drive, and other forms of removable media require access to the outside of the case, while internal hard drives can be mounted anywhere in the case that is within reach of data and power cables. *See also* external drive.

IP address: The Internet Protocol address is expressed as an identifying number for sites, devices, or users on an Internet (or on a TCP/IP network used to connect local computers together).

ISP: Internet service provider. A company or organization that sells access to the Internet to users.

jumper: A small metal clip within a plastic block that is placed on metal pins to turn on or off a specific function or to make a particular setting.

K: Kilo, as in 1,000.

Kb: Kilobit; 1,024 bits.

KB: Kilobyte; 1,024 bytes.

Kbps: Kilobits per second.

KBps: Kilobytes per second.

kernel: The most basic, essential element of the operating system, loaded first and kept in memory.

LAN: Local area network. A connection between two or more computers at a location.

laser printer: A printer that produces pages based on electronic signals from a computer. The dots of an image are converted into a laser beam that imparts a charge to paper that attracts dry ink that is later fused in place by heat.

local area network: *See* LAN.

main memory: Another term for conventional memory.

Mb: *See* megabit.

MB: *See* megabyte.

Mbps: Megabits per second. The number of bits, in millions, moved in one second.

MBps: Megabytes per second. The number of bytes, in millions, moved in one second.

MBR: *See* master boot record.

media: A physical device that stores computer-generated data. Floppy disks and hard disks are magnetic media. CD-ROMs are optical media.

megabit: A million bits. In reference to memory, equals 1,048,576 bits. Expressed as Mb.

megabyte: A million bytes. In reference to memory, equals 1,048,576 bytes. Expressed as MB.

memory: The part of a computer that remembers 0s and 1s. Unlike human memory, it cannot remember any context.

memory refresh: *See* refresh.

microprocessor: The part of the computer that processes. In microcomputers, the chip that actually executes instructions and manipulates information. Also called the CPU or the processor.

monitor: A video display.

motherboard: The main board of the PC, holding the microprocessor, system BIOS, expansion slots, and other critical components.

mouse: A device used to control the location of an onscreen pointer that identifies data or issues commands to the processor.

MSDOS.SYS: A file that is the essential element of the boot files for Microsoft operating systems from DOS through Windows 98. (In IBM's version of DOS, a similar file is called IBMDOS.COM.)

MTBF: Mean Time Between Failure. A measure by hardware manufacturers that purports to show the average time a component can be expected to work before it fails.

multicore processor: A microprocessor that includes two or more independent processors within the same physical chip, permitting certain applications to execute multiple processes at the same time.

nano (n): One billionth. A nanosecond is abbreviated as *ns*.

NIC: Network Interface Card. An adapter that permits a device to connect to an Ethernet for the exchange of information and commands.

nonvolatile memory: Memory that does not need to be refreshed. Therefore, it doesn't require much power. CMOS RAM is a form of nonvolatile memory.

null modem cable: A specialized serial cable used to connect two serial devices directly, without the use of a modem.

operating system (OS): A program that enables a computer to load programs and that controls the screen, the drives, and other devices. Microsoft's DOS was used in early systems through Windows 95/98 and ME; Windows 2000 and Windows XP use new code that performs the same functions.

OverDrive CPU: An add-on chip from Intel for upgrading a PC with a faster and/or more powerful CPU.

overvoltage protection: In a power supply, a circuit that shuts down the device if the output voltage exceeds a specified limit.

parallel port: The I/O channel to a parallel device, such as a printer.

password check option: A feature of some ROM BIOS systems, it can be used to prevent unauthorized use of the system or alterations to the setup.

PC Card: The Personal Computer Memory Card International Association specification for a credit-card-sized addition to PCs, most often used in portable computers.

PCMCIA: *See* PC Card.

peripheral: A hardware device connected to a computer. Typical peripherals include keyboards, monitors, printers, disk drives, and more.

pinout: A drawing or table that lists the nature of the signals that use particular pins of a chip or connector.

platter: The rotating disk within a hard disk drive used to hold data.

Plug-and-Play: A new device plugged into such a system would be able to set its own IRQ, DMA channel, I/O port setting, and memory addresses while avoiding conflicts with other peripherals' settings.

POST: Power-On Self-Test. The BIOS ROM contains a series of hardware tests that runs each time a computer is turned on. If hardware errors are found, POST either beeps or displays error messages.

processor: The part of the computer that executes instructions and manipulates information. In microcomputers, this is a single chip. It is also called a CPU or a microprocessor.

protected mode: The mode of an 80286 or later microprocessor in which the processor can address extended memory and protect OS memory from direct manipulation by applications. *See also* virtual memory.

quad-core processor: *See* multicore processor.

RAM: Random Access Memory. Any part of this memory can be used by the microprocessor. Each storage location in RAM has a unique address, and each address can be either written to or read by the processor. In DOS, conventional memory, maximum 640K, is the area used to hold DOS, applications, and data. Expanded memory and extended memory are also RAM. When people use the term RAM casually (as in "How much RAM does your computer have?"), they're usually talking about conventional memory, plus expanded and extended memory. Windows, unlike DOS, uses both conventional memory and extended memory.

reboot: To restart the computer. *See also* boot, cold boot, and warm boot.

refresh: Dynamic memory (DRAM) forgets the information it holds unless it is rewritten regularly. Memory with a faster refresh rate responds quicker. Refresh rate also is another term for the vertical scan frequency of a monitor.

register: One of several cells in a processor that is used to manipulate data. For example, a CPU can load a value from memory into a register, load another value into another register, add the two values together and put the result in a third register, and then copy the third register's value to a location in memory.

registry: An essential component of Windows 95/98 and later versions holding the system configuration files including settings, preferences, and information about installed hardware and software.

resolution: A measure of the sharpness or granularity of an image or monitor, usually expressed as a number of horizontal pixels multiplied by a number of vertical pixels.

ribbon cable: A flat multiconductor cable used primarily under the covers of the computer to connect peripheral devices, such as disk drives to controllers.

RIMM: A module for Rambus memory.

RJ-11: The male connector on a telephone cable, usually with four wires, that mates with a wall port or the input port on a telephone modem.

RJ-45: The male connector on an Ethernet cable, with as many as eight wires. It is similar in appearance to an RJ-11, but slightly larger and incompatible.

ROM: Read Only Memory. Recorded once, at the factory, ROM is the ideal way to hold instructions that should never change, such as the instructions your computer requires to access the disk drive. *See also* BIOS and RAM.

ROM address: The memory address location within a ROM chip, often used to mean the first address.

ROM BIOS: *See* BIOS.

router: A device that connects network hubs together. A valuable modern router includes a firewall to prevent unwanted intrusion by hackers.

scanner: A device that converts printed or written text or illustrations into a digital file that can be manipulated by the computer. A modern optical character recognition application can convert text in the digital image into characters than can be worked with by a word processor.

SDRAM: Synchronous Dynamic Random Access Memory. An advanced form of dynamic RAM memory that can be synchronized with the processor's clock, eliminating wait states and latency.

Serial ATA (SATA): A standard for interfacing computers to storage devices such as hard drives and DVD drives. SATA version 1 is capable of 1.5 Gbps, however the standard is scalable to 2x (3 Gbps) and 4x (6 Gbps).

server: A computer or other device that manages a component of a network. A file server holds shared files; a print server manages printers, and a network server controls communication functions of the network.

setup: A program used to store hardware configuration information in the CMOS chip of a modern machine.

shadowing: A method to improve performance of a computer by copying some or all of the contents of ROM to faster RAM.

SIMM: Single Inline Memory Modules are units that can hold a group of individual memory chips — typically eight or nine — in a single unit that plugs into a socket. A common current design is the 72-pin SIMM, which can hold from 1 to 64MB, delivered in a single 32-bit data path.

single user: An operating system that allows only one user to use the computer at a time.

single user, multitask: A version of single user that allows only one user to perform multiple tasks simultaneously. Examples include OS/2, Windows 3.1, and VM/386. *See also* single user.

single user, single task: A version of single user that allows only one user at a time to do one task at a time. DOS is an example.

SRAM: Static Random Access Memory chips that do not require refresh as long as they are powered.

state: Condition, as in On-Off, High-Low, or Zero-One. In computers, this means the particular way that all memory locations, registers, and logic gates are set. State is also used casually to indicate the particular condition and status of the computer.

surface mount: A circuit-board design in which chips are directly attached to the board instead of being soldered in pin holes or attached through sockets. In theory, a surface mount design is less susceptible to problems caused by bad connections. However, a failed chip often requires replacement of the entire circuit board.

surge protector: A device to protect electrical components from damage caused by overvoltage (surges). A more sophisticated uninterruptible power supply (UPS) also protects against undervoltage (brownouts) and a short power outage.

system: The memory in the computer that DOS (or the chosen operating system) can use for the OS, applications, and data. On most DOS computers, this is also called conventional memory, and it has a maximum memory of 640K. DOS 5.0 and later versions, and DR DOS 6.0 can also use high memory (the first 64K of extended memory), so these operating systems have an effective system memory of 704K.

system boot parameters: Many BIOS chips permit the user to specify a number of options at boot.

system files: The hidden files necessary to boot the operating system.

SYSTEM.INI: A Windows file that contains information about the hardware environment.

tower: An upright case for a computer.

transfer rate: The amount of data, measured in bytes per second, that a computer can read from or write to a device, such as a hard disk, a modem, or a network.

twisted pair: A cabling design that uses two thin unshielded wires twisted around each other to somewhat reduce interference. Twisted-pair cables are used for telephones and basic Ethernet local area networks. More sophisticated systems use coaxial or fiber optic cables, which are more expensive and difficult to install.

uninterruptible power supply (UPS): A device that combines a surge protector, a large battery, and electronic circuitry to shield a PC or other system from surges, undervoltages, and short power outages.

upper memory: Memory located between 640K and 1,024K (1MB).

URL: Uniform Resource Locator. An Internet address system.

USB: Universal Serial Bus. The high-speed external bus that allows easy connection and removal of devices while a computer is running. The original specifications of USB 1.0 and USB 1.1 have been supplanted by the considerably faster USB 2.0 model.

virtual memory: A means to enable a system to work with a larger memory than it is permitted to use or with a memory that is larger than the memory that actually exists. Paged memory is one type of virtual memory.

virus: A piece of code that corrupts your PC without your permission or knowledge.

warm boot: Restarting a computer without turning off the power or pressing the hardware reset button; that is, using the Ctrl+Alt+Delete combination. See also cold boot.

Zip drive: A popular design for a large-capacity removable storage device, holding 100 or 250MB on a platter about the size of a floppy disk.

Index

• *X* •

Business/Accounting & Bookkeeping

Bookkeeping For Dummies
978-0-7645-9848-7

eBay Business
All-in-One For Dummies,
2nd Edition
978-0-470-38536-4

Job Interviews
For Dummies,
3rd Edition
978-0-470-17748-8

Resumes For Dummies,
5th Edition
978-0-470-08037-5

Stock Investing
For Dummies,
3rd Edition
978-0-470-40114-9

Successful Time
Management
For Dummies
978-0-470-29034-7

Computer Hardware

BlackBerry For Dummies,
3rd Edition
978-0-470-45762-7

Computers For Seniors
For Dummies
978-0-470-24055-7

iPhone For Dummies,
2nd Edition
978-0-470-42342-4

Laptops For Dummies,
3rd Edition
978-0-470-27759-1

Macs For Dummies,
10th Edition
978-0-470-27817-8

Cooking & Entertaining

Cooking Basics
For Dummies,
3rd Edition
978-0-7645-7206-7

Wine For Dummies,
4th Edition
978-0-470-04579-4

Diet & Nutrition

Dieting For Dummies,
2nd Edition
978-0-7645-4149-0

Nutrition For Dummies,
4th Edition
978-0-471-79868-2

Weight Training
For Dummies,
3rd Edition
978-0-471-76845-6

Digital Photography

Digital Photography
For Dummies,
6th Edition
978-0-470-25074-7

Photoshop Elements 7
For Dummies
978-0-470-39700-8

Gardening

Gardening Basics
For Dummies
978-0-470-03749-2

Organic Gardening
For Dummies,
2nd Edition
978-0-470-43067-5

Green/Sustainable

Green Building
& Remodeling
For Dummies
978-0-470-17559-0

Green Cleaning
For Dummies
978-0-470-39106-8

Green IT For Dummies
978-0-470-38688-0

Health

Diabetes For Dummies,
3rd Edition
978-0-470-27086-8

Food Allergies
For Dummies
978-0-470-09584-3

Living Gluten-Free
For Dummies
978-0-471-77383-2

Hobbies/General

Chess For Dummies,
2nd Edition
978-0-7645-8404-6

Drawing For Dummies
978-0-7645-5476-6

Knitting For Dummies,
2nd Edition
978-0-470-28747-7

Organizing For Dummies
978-0-7645-5300-4

SuDoku For Dummies
978-0-470-01892-7

Home Improvement

Energy Efficient Homes
For Dummies
978-0-470-37602-7

Home Theater
For Dummies,
3rd Edition
978-0-470-41189-6

Living the Country Lifestyle
All-in-One For Dummies
978-0-470-43061-3

Solar Power Your Home
For Dummies
978-0-470-17569-9

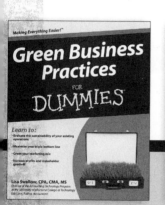

Internet

Blogging For Dummies,
2nd Edition
978-0-470-23017-6

eBay For Dummies,
6th Edition
978-0-470-49741-8

Facebook For Dummies
978-0-470-26273-3

Google Blogger
For Dummies
978-0-470-40742-4

Web Marketing
For Dummies,
2nd Edition
978-0-470-37181-7

WordPress For Dummies,
2nd Edition
978-0-470-40296-2

Language & Foreign Language

French For Dummies
978-0-7645-5193-2

Italian Phrases
For Dummies
978-0-7645-7203-6

Spanish For Dummies
978-0-7645-5194-9

Spanish For Dummies,
Audio Set
978-0-470-09585-0

Macintosh

Mac OS X Snow Leopard
For Dummies
978-0-470-43543-4

Math & Science

Algebra I For Dummies
978-0-7645-5325-7

Biology For Dummies
978-0-7645-5326-4

Calculus For Dummies
978-0-7645-2498-1

Chemistry For Dummies
978-0-7645-5430-8

Microsoft Office

Excel 2007 For Dummies
978-0-470-03737-9

Office 2007 All-in-One
Desk Reference
For Dummies
978-0-471-78279-7

Music

Guitar For Dummies,
2nd Edition
978-0-7645-9904-0

iPod & iTunes
For Dummies,
6th Edition
978-0-470-39062-7

Piano Exercises
For Dummies
978-0-470-38765-8

Parenting & Education

Parenting For Dummies,
2nd Edition
978-0-7645-5418-6

Type 1 Diabetes
For Dummies
978-0-470-17811-9

Pets

Cats For Dummies,
2nd Edition
978-0-7645-5275-5

Dog Training For Dummies,
2nd Edition
978-0-7645-8418-3

Puppies For Dummies,
2nd Edition
978-0-470-03717-1

Religion & Inspiration

The Bible For Dummies
978-0-7645-5296-0

Catholicism For Dummies
978-0-7645-5391-2

Women in the Bible
For Dummies
978-0-7645-8475-6

Self-Help & Relationship

Anger Management
For Dummies
978-0-470-03715-7

Overcoming Anxiety
For Dummies
978-0-7645-5447-6

Sports

Baseball For Dummies,
3rd Edition
978-0-7645-7537-2

Basketball For Dummies,
2nd Edition
978-0-7645-5248-9

Golf For Dummies,
3rd Edition
978-0-471-76871-5

Web Development

Web Design All-in-One
For Dummies
978-0-470-41796-6

Windows Vista

Windows Vista
For Dummies
978-0-471-75421-3

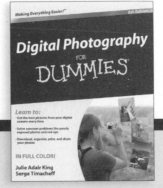